The Modern World

THE MODERN WORLD

NORBERT LYNTON

Head of the School of Art History and General Studies,
Chelsea School of Art, London

McGRAW-HILL BOOK COMPANY
NEW YORK · TORONTO

General Editors

BERNARD S. MYERS   TREWIN COPPLESTONE
New York   *London*

PREHISTORIC AND PRIMITIVE MAN
Dr Andreas Lommel, Director of the Museum of Ethnology, Munich

THE ANCIENT WORLD
Professor Giovanni Garbini, Institute of Near Eastern Studies, University of Rome

THE CLASSICAL WORLD
Dr Donald Strong, Assistant Keeper, Department of Greek and Roman Antiquities, British Museum, London

THE EARLY CHRISTIAN AND BYZANTINE WORLD
Professor Jean Lassus, Institute of Art and Archaeology, University of Paris

THE WORLD OF ISLAM
Dr Ernst J. Grube, Associate Curator in Charge, Islamic Department, Metropolitan Museum of Art, New York

THE ORIENTAL WORLD
Jeannine Auboyer, Keeper at the Musée Guimet, Paris
Dr Roger Goepper, Director of the Department of Oriental Art, State Museums, Berlin

THE MEDIEVAL WORLD
Peter Kidson, Conway Librarian, Courtauld Institute of Art, London

MAN AND THE RENAISSANCE
Andrew Martindale, Senior Lecturer in the School of Fine Arts, University of East Anglia

THE AGE OF BAROQUE
Michael Kitson, Lecturer in the History of Art, Courtauld Institute of Art, London

THE MODERN WORLD
Norbert Lynton, Head of the School of Art History and General Studies, Chelsea School of Art, London

Library of Congress Catalog Card Number 65-21593
39260

© PAUL HAMLYN LIMITED 1965

PRINTED IN THE NETHERLANDS BY JOH. ENSCHEDÉ EN ZONEN
GRAFISCHE INRICHTING N.V.   HAARLEM

List of Contents

Colour Plates

Paul Cézanne: *Self-portrait*. Pencil sketch. 8¾ × 5 in. (22 × 12.5 cm.).
Courtesy Art Institute of Chicago. Arthur Heun Fund.

Introduction

It is precisely our uncertainty which brings us a good deal closer to reality than was possible in former periods which had faith in the absolute.   KARL MANNHEIM

Today we are in a position to survey a vast field of artistic creation. We are familiar with the art of distant periods and people and know a great deal about the circumstances in which widely divergent kinds of art were produced. Though we have our predilections, we are accustomed to the notion of different kinds of beauty and different forms of significance and feel no need for a universally accepted hierarchy of art forms and styles.

In the eighteenth century the situation was quite different. Though artists in the western world might take liberties with the principles they had inherited, these principles were still upheld and defended. Rococo painting obviously represented some deviation from the high seriousness exemplified in the work of Raphael and preached by the academies ever since the sixteenth century, but it did not challenge this idealism. Not that there were no arguments about the relative greatness of modern and ancient artists, or about the primacy of colour over drawing or of drawing over colour (represented in France as a posthumous rivalry between Rubens and Poussin), but such dissensions took place within one small area, as it now seems to us, of the field of art.

Taking the period from the High Renaissance to Tiepolo as a whole, it is clear that the most highly regarded artists were those who stood at the centre of art, embodying those values upon which art was believed to be founded. Today we honour more readily those artists who are seen to stand on the periphery of art, seeking to extend its realm. This reversal has come about during the last century and a half; it was made possible and necessary by revolutionary processes that were initiated in the eighteenth century.

To speak of that century as an age of reason is curiously wide of the mark. It opened as an age of reasonableness and became an age of revolution. The world as described by Descartes and Newton seemed to offer man a definable and secure place. All would be well if man lived in harmony with this essentially harmonious universe—a beneficent God-ordained system into which man would fit if he practised a kind of spiritual etiquette based on moderation. But having settled his relationship with his Maker, man now turned to himself. 'The proper study of mankind is man,' wrote Pope, the greatest poet to celebrate this ordered universe, and in so writing he struck at its foundations. Using that marvellous reason, which had achieved so much for preceding generations, eighteenth-century men probed into man himself. Being able to take for granted the physical and theological pattern left to them, they examined man for the first time independently of any supernatural factors: man as man. At once it was seen that reason plays a minor role in man's life. He has emotions, sensations, instincts that determine his actions and reactions; even when reason is put to work, irrational factors will decide what it

is to work on. Pascal's precocious recognition that 'the heart has its reasons of which reason knows nothing' suddenly became a commonplace. And when man turned to the society that shaped his life, he found it ill-designed to meet his needs. Yet what is society's purpose?

Jean-Jacques Rousseau (1712–78) asked most of the questions that his age wanted asked and provided many answers. He examined civilised society and found it to be a kind of straitjacket that hampered man's natural growth. But society was clearly created by men, for their mutual benefit in some far distant past. If some were placed in positions of power, this must have been by general agreement and for the good of all. So it follows that if rulers failed to govern benifically, the implicit contract which had given them their special position could be considered broken and new arrangements made. Accepting the ancient dream of a Golden Age when all men lived in perfect harmony, and writing at a time when colonial developments were making Europeans more aware of other forms of society, Rousseau dreamt of a primitive society devoid of the artificial accretions that seemed to stifle his world. For the first time in the history of civilisation man wondered what he might have lost in achieving social order and material advantages. And as he turned away from civilisation and looked longingly towards what had been thought of as barbarism, so also he turned away from cities and formal gardens towards nature.

Nature came to be seen as the regenerative, corrective influence it has been to us ever since. For the first time man felt the exhilerating drama offered by great mountains and the hints of cosmic vastness and timelessness given by deserts and empty oceans. It is difficult for us today to imagine a world in which people took no interest in wild nature, but it has to be emphasised that to European culture the high and slightly guilty regard we have for landscape and for the rustic and the seafaring life is something quite recent. Nor do the occasional exceptions in earlier times disprove this—one thinks of Petrarch's ascent of Mont Ventoux in 1336 and of Breughel's Alpine sketches of 1554. The writers of the later eighteenth century and the painters of the nineteenth educated the western world into a sensibility towards the appearance and the processes of nature. And this last aspect is perhaps the more important: it was not only the appearance of nature that now appealed to man, but he also came to regard wild nature as the exemplar of life and death and of creativity. At the same time science dramatically developed its ability to explain these processes in nature and in man himself.

Developments of this kind, accompanying the demolition of old social structures, the industrial revolution's assault on old ways of life and the loosening hold of religious faith on the minds of many, have given us a sense of vulnerability and of individual isolation as well as a new need for self-reliance. Modern man is expected not so much to learn the rules of religion and society and to abide by them, as to 'find himself' and to be 'true to himself'. The onus is inescapable and considerable, and it is small wonder if, in all forms of human creativity, the kind of beauty that results from arranging beautiful objects to convey a harmonious idea has generally been replaced by more challenging and discordant forms of signification.

Revolutions in attitudes and values, unlike political revolutions, proceed mostly below the surface of man's actions. Obviously the nineteenth and twentieth century world is full of elements, even apart from the constancies of human existence, inherited from the eighteenth. This cultural retentiveness is what makes history like a woollen thread and not a string of sausages, varying in quality and degree from country to country, from town to country, between social classes. A survey like this one must highlight those new elements that establish themselves sufficiently firmly to become part of the complex thread, and it is the beginning of each significant fibre that is likely to receive the most attention. The reader is therefore warned against seeing as a succession of inspired leaps those gestures of rebellion and reconstruction that may scarcely have been noticeable within the matted complexities of the contemporary situation. Certainly the nineteenth century holds a special place in history for offering the widest chasms between progressives and reactionaries, rich and poor, enlightened and philistine. Any revolution separates clearly those who wish to preserve what they can of the past from those who want to replace the past with something new. In the nineteenth century this confrontation happened at many levels of existence: radicalism and conservatism divided the worlds of religion, politics, science, and education as much as the world of the arts. The vehemence of the struggle was quite unprecedented.

The eighteenth century, then, prepared the ground for these battles and largely determined the causes over which they should be fought. In the arts it had been a strange period. The seventeenth century, the age of Baroque, had been full of creative actions on a bold scale. Splendid buildings were erected in Europe's capitals, especially churches and palaces, but including also the handsome merchant houses of Amsterdam. There was an impressive series of outstanding artists from several countries—Bernini, Poussin, Rubens, Rembrandt, Velasquez, and behind them crowds of other fine painters, sculptors and architects that in a less star-spangled age might have achieved greater prominence. The arts had worked together harmoniously to create monuments to the glory of God and of kings and princes: the palace of the sun-king Louis XIV at Versailles is a fitting climax to the age. The eighteenth century was

not without its extravagant princes trying to emulate Versailles (especially in Germany where, in other respects too, the Baroque had a late flowering), but the art of that age is characterised by delicacy where the Baroque was robust, domesticity where the Baroque was palatial, privacy where the Baroque was public. The virtues of eighteenth-century art are those of restraint and refinement, and this restraint applies also to art's subject-matter and emotional content. The novel, the essay and the shorter poem are its literary forms while the seventeenth century had produced great epic poems and real tragedies. The scale of creativity had changed. Although the academies continued to yield pride of place to history painting (paintings of subjects from ancient mythology and history, from the Bible and very occasionally from modern literature), it was the minor art of portraiture that flourished particularly. When eighteenth-century artists attempted the great themes to which they were encouraged to aspire, they diminished them, as Boucher, for all the charm of his art, diminished the gods and goddesses that lounge about his elegant canvases. The seventeenth century had been heroic in its actions; so too in less obvious ways the nineteenth century was to be heroic. In the seventeenth century this heroism had the almost invariable support of great patronage; in the nineteenth, heroic actions were to be performed increasingly without benefit of patronage or encouragement.

The eighteenth century left much in confusion, not least the arts. The habit of preaching one kind of art and producing another weakened the principles upon which art had been founded. But the century saw also processes beginning that would be much more destructive: the growth of historicism, of archaeology and of interest in non-European civilisations. The Greco-Roman paintings discovered at Pompeii and Herculaneum, the detailed study and recording, for the first time, of classical Greek architecture in Athens and elsewhere, and of Roman architecture in outlying centres such as Palmyra and Baalbek, the investigation of medieval remains as part of the study of national pasts—these were some of the most important aspects. They led inevitably to the dethronement of imperial Rome and sixteenth-century Italy as the only true authorities in art. Greek architecture had qualities which the Roman had not, imperial Roman architecture of Augustus's time was shown to be only one stage in the development of Roman design, countries such as Britain, France and Germany could point to exceptional artistic achievements completed before the Renaissance spread its veneer of Mediterranean classicism, and the arts of Egypt, India and the Far East offered exotic delights as well as serious instruction. Where there had been one composite model for high art, there now were many. It is remarkable how quickly writers on art and sometimes artists found it necessary to discover moral reasons rather than aesthetic ones for attaching themselves to one style of art or another.

One aspect of this intensified interest in the past and awakening appreciation of other cultures was the development of art history. Before the second half of the eighteenth century the art of the past was studied in direct proportion to its significance as a guide to the present. Vasari in the sixteenth century had written biographies of the most important artists of his country, from Giotto to Michelangelo, to show how in Michelangelo Italy had produced an artist at least equal to the greatest in antiquity. Of antiquity itself he knew relatively little; of the Dark Ages that came between his time and antiquity he did not care to know much. Imperial Rome was the only past that mattered. From the 1760s on this simply focussed view has to be discarded. The German scholar, Winckelmann, made the first systematic study of Greek art and showed how different phases in its development brought forth different qualities comparable to those discernible in the different phases of Renaissance art. This implied what others at about the same time had stated firmly—that criteria must vary according to the period of art to which they are applied. Other scholars made studies of Byzantine painting, found opposed virtues in Sienese and Florentine painting, and came to see qualities in the 'primitive' phase of Italian art (particularly in the art of Fra Angelico), that were not to be found in the more grandiose art of Raphael. This acceptance of the relativity of styles brought with it the separation of aesthetic quality from the idiom, and to some extent from the subject-matter of any particular work of art.

The nineteenth-century artist was freed of all obligations but that of being a genius. In his essay on Gothic architecture, inspired by the sight of Strasbourg Cathedral (1772), Goethe states that 'whether it proceeds from savage rudeness, or from refined feeling, art is complete and vital. It is the art of the characteristic, the only true art. The genius must look neither at models nor rules, must not profit by the wings of others, but by his own'. And Baudelaire warned him (1859): 'Everything that is not sublime is useless and criminal'. The freedom thus given to the artist is matched only by the burden placed on him. And on us too there is placed a burden, to search into the world of the artist which never before has had so many mansions, but the rewards are infinite.

The numbers in the margins refer to the illustrations: heavy type for colour plates, italics for black and white illustrations.

The First Half of
the Nineteenth Century

DAVID AND NEO-CLASSICAL PAINTING

In 1785, the *Salon*, the official annual Paris art exhibition, was dominated by a picture at once recognised as revolu-
1 tionary: *The Oath of the Horatii*, by Jacques Louis David (1748–1825). A critic called it 'the most beautiful picture of the century'. Yet it is a curiously bare work, charmless in colour and austere in design—scarcely the kind of picture one would have thought likely to please the fashionable world of eighteenth-century France. In fact, it met a demand that had been growing during the preceding twenty or thirty years for an art that refutes the grace and frivolity of the Rococo and aims at high standards of didactic seriousness and aesthetic severity. Others, such as Greuze and David's teacher Vien, had set off in this direction but here was a work that fully satisfied both standards. Its subject is that moment when the brothers swear to fight to the death to save their city from the attacking tyrant, and David has staged it with the strictest economy and clarity. The three young men are fused into one silhouette, balanced on the right by the looser group of women and children. All the figures and the action occupy one plane within the bare and box-like space of the picture's architecture. The result is great psychological concentration on the event. Stylistically, this picture derives from Roman reliefs and the paintings of Poussin, although David goes much further in constructing his composition on almost blatantly geometrical lines. Behind the impressiveness of the subject stands the condition of France. France was on the eve of revolution; and here was a picture celebrating the moral vigour of republican Rome.

In subsequent pictures David returned again and again to themes that were drawn from ancient history to illuminate the condition of France. His style became more elaborate and he used the latest archaeological discoveries to produce an effect of historical accuracy. The ladies of Paris began to imitate the clothes and coiffures of the women in his pictures; French furniture makers drew on his pictures and on his sources. David became politically as well as culturally powerful, and acted as artistic dictator until the fall of Robespierre, when he was imprisoned for some months. It was then that he conceived the theme for a
2 picture to celebrate peace and love: *The Sabine Women* (1796–9), showing these ill-gotten women boldly imposing peace between their captor-husbands and their fathers and former husbands. The picture transcended political factions and was greatly admired. David himself saw it as a great advance from the primitive solidity of the *Horatii*, and as Greek where the earlier picture had been essentially Roman. He modelled the main figures on the Hellenistic sculptures that General Bonaparte was sending to France from Italy, and left his fighting men unclothed in the Greek

manner. Poussin is still behind the general character of the composition, but again David concentrated attention firmly on the main action, and abstracted the crowd and their setting on firm and geometrical lines.

With works such as these David made Neo-Classicism a revolutionary style, taking it far beyond sixteenth- and seventeenth-century classicism in factual accuracy, severity of presentation and undisguised didacticism. What also separates Neo-Classicism from Renaissance classicism, and illustrates the predicament of all art at the beginning of the Romantic age, is the air of artificiality that hangs over even the best efforts of David and his followers. At the moment of the High Renaissance the exceptionally highly developed classicism of Raphael looks like a natural growth out of the art of his time aided by special circumstances and personal inclinations, and much the same is true of Poussin's move into classicism within the broad stream of Baroque art. But David's classicism was not inherited from Vien, the effect of whose teaching had been rather to diminish classicism in David's eyes. 'The antique will not seduce me', he said in 1774, when he set off for Rome; 'it lacks action and does not stir the emotions'. What he saw in Rome persuaded him to *choose* classicism, and his success led others to choose the style soon after. The cult of archaeological accuracy served to underline this artificiality. Stylistic questions apart, Neo-Classicism in David's hands also served to cleanse painting of a lavishness of design and colour that in the hands of all but the finest painters had become cloying. In his portraits David could achieve an astonishing directness in which stylistic elements play relatively little part. When he worked as chief painter to Napoleon—when, that is, he acted as court painter to a great ruler and so found himself in a position like that held by some of the great Baroque painters—David could approach the Baroque in grandiloquence and splendour. His large *Coronation* (1802–7), showing Napoleon crowning Josephine as Empress, bridges the vast gap between the enthusiastic portrayals of royal pomp of the Baroque and the more prosaic court-portraits of Victorian times. David was, in fact, interested in a wide range of art, studying Rubens particularly in order to lighten his palette. As France's leading painter he had a large number of select students, and he taught them with a liberality of taste that was quite unusual in Neo-Classical circles.

INGRES

His most successful pupils were Antoine Jean Gros, whose dramatic pictures of Napoleon campaigning have much of the Baroque's fulsomness, while his teaching was much more strictly classical than David's, and Jean Auguste Dominique Ingres (1780–1867), who upheld the dignity and the primacy of Neo-Classicism in France during the

12

1. **Jean Auguste Dominique Ingres.**
Jupiter and Thetis. 1811. Oil on canvas.
130¾ × 101¼ in. (332 × 257 cm.).
Musée Granet, Aix-en-Provence.
Though a convinced classicist, Ingres
embodied in his work instinctive leanings
to the exotic and the primitive.

first half of the nineteenth century while working in a highly idiosyncratic style shot through with Romantic fantasy. In him are uniquely combined the two main traditions of French painting, that of Poussin and that of Rubens, with Poussin representing rationalism, design and an appeal to the educated mind, and Rubens emotionalism, colour and an appeal to the senses. Consciously he was dominated by classical standards. His devotion to the ancients was absolute: 'Regarding the marvels of the ancients, doubt itself is a reproach'. He taught that all the expressive power of painting resided in the drawing. Drawing 'is the foundation, it is everything. A thing well enough drawn is always well enough painted'. He accepted the high academic rating of history painting, and, while it was necessary for him to paint portraits (and they include some of his finest work), landscape was to him at best a backdrop. He advised a visiting German landscape painter: 'Study Phidias, Raphael and Beethoven, and you will be the greatest landscape painter in the world'. Colour was to him 'the animal part of art', a dangerous element that could interfere with 'the profound study that the great purity of form demands'. Purity of form demands purity of outline. Ingres's drawing abandons the meticulously detailed modelling of academic drawing since Raphael in favour of an outline that will

include, by its absolute truth, the roundness of the object. The Greeks were thought to have placed a similar emphasis on the outline, and the published engravings of discoveries at Pompeii, and Herculaneum may have encouraged this notion. But Ingres's line went beyond the normal drawing of Neo-Classicism in its ability to present a highly refined form and yet transmit his sensual awareness of the subject.

Partly because of this, his work was at first dismissed as barbaric. Ingres did in fact find himself attracted by what he described as 'the formless beginnings of certain arts' which 'sometimes contain, fundamentally, more perfection than the perfected art'. He is the first primitivist in European painting, studying Giotto and early Florentine painting as well as unclassical aspects of ancient art as found in some Greek vase painting.

His *Jupiter and Thetis* (1811) illustrates the dualism of his art. At first sight it is a boldly Neo-Classical work, clearly organised on one plane and with the concentration of action that David's example encouraged. But to convey the emotional situation described by Homer, the clinging and beseeching Thetis and Zeus obdurate, he has recourse to an extreme degree of exaggeration and abstraction, opposing a soft, curling, structureless form to an almost symmetrical monolith. In due course, however, Ingres established himself as the defender of classical standards with paintings in which his idiosyncracies were subdued; he had a tremendously successful career and honours were heaped on him. He ruled despotically over a large number of students, forbidding them absolutely to look at pictures by Rubens and attempted to rid French art of all the tendencies associated with Romanticism. In his own work it continues, however, to be his hypersensitivity to line and the powerful sensuality expressing itself through that line, that makes his work so much superior to most Neo-Classicism and most Romanticism. His work ranged brilliantly from exquisitely composed portraits to sensuous paintings of nude women as *Odalisques*, their erotic content sharpened by exotic seasoning, and from limp and defenceless maidens chained to rocks for semi-Gothic Rogers to rescue, to *The Apotheosis of Homer*, intended to decorate a ceiling and representing an apotheosis of classicism, with portraits of the heroes of the French classical tradition. One of his last works was *The Turkish Bath* (1863), an anthology of his life-long studies of the female form, assembled as though to prove his command of abstract design.

Ingres, by placing himself at the head of French classicism and attacking all aspects of Romanticism, labelled himself a reactionary. Yet he has given much to modern art and in many respects comes closer to later developments than most of his liberal contemporaries. Not only have Degas, Picasso and others looked to him as a master draughtsman, but his reiterated emphasis on drawing combined with his sense of perfect form is abstract in intention. Classical idealism aims at the representation of the perfect object; Ingres's idealism aims at the perfect work of art. For its sake he allowed himself extremes of distortion of forms and of space, and this not for the sake of any impersonal absolute but for the sake of the expressive power of each picture. His work varies widely. Even his bigotry has something modern about it: no painter had more moral view of art and of the rightness of his own work. And he is the first painter to voice his sense of the frivolousness of easel painting, that 'invention of periods of decadence'—a view frequently expressed since his time. If his rejection of colour marks him as an opponent of the element that becomes the spearhead of the revolution in painting, this too must be seen in part as an aspect of his process of abstraction, especially at a time when colour must have seemed an inseparable part of modelling and chiaroscuro, both of them enemies of form as he saw it.

DELACROIX

As leader of classicism, Ingres found himself confronted by the younger painter, Eugène Delacroix (1798–1863), as the unwilling champion of Romanticism and modernity. Ingres consciously held classical values while he undermined them in his art; Delacroix resisted being called Romantic and saw himself as part of the classical tradition. His view of that tradition was a personal one. He greatly admired Poussin and indeed wrote about him. But his opinions changed, for having admired Raphael as the greatest of all painters (Ingres would have agreed with him), he replaces him in turn with Rubens, Titian and Rembrandt. The 'ancients' were his ideal of excellence, but 'Titian and the Flemish painters have the spirit of the Antique', and 'Rubens is more Homeric than some of the ancients'. At every stage of his work the classical and the romantic conflict and collaborate. Baudelaire said that 'Delacroix was passionately in love with passion, but coldly determined to express passion as clearly as possible', and at once we recognise that this synthesis of passion and control is the basis of all the greatest art. But as a Romantic Delacroix placed special value on excitement, warmth, richness, spontaneity and fantasy even while he insisted on the need for knowledge and skill.

As a young man, Delacroix had greatly admired the work of Théodore Géricault (1791–1824). From him he got his [4] passion for English painting and English literature (particularly Byron and Scott), and his first major work, *Dante and Virgil crossing the Styx* (1822), owes a good deal to Géricault. But Delacroix found his friend's work lacking in unity. To him unity meant a deep concordance of subject, meaning and manner, and the integration of the elements of the picture into one dynamic gesture. He was, in short, a Baroque painter, bringing to largely secular subjects the celebratory enthusiasm which the Baroque reserved for gods and kings. Medieval history and legends, Nordic myths, Renaissance and modern fiction, contemporary events and scenes—Delacroix ranged widely over the subject-matter that the age of Romanticism opened to art. His first masterpiece, *The Massacre of Scio* (1824), symbolically represents the dominant political topic of his time, the Greeks' struggle for independence, and he returns to the theme in *Greece expiring on the ruins of Missolonghi* (1827). The 1830 revolution even led him to produce his one treatment of contemporary Parisian life, though this too was in symbolical terms—*Liberty on the Barricades*. More characteristic of him, though, is subject-matter of a more melancholy kind, reflecting more directly his own personality and solitude. We may imagine him in character somewhere between Hamlet and Faust, both of them very much in his mind and frequently in his art. Perhaps *The Death of Sardanapalus* (1828) reveals him most fully. Its subject comes, like many others, from English literature, from Byron's tragedy of 1821, [2,5] dedicated to the author of *Faust*. The Oriental king is soon to die. He reclines on his funeral pyre, while the objects that gladdened his life are destroyed before his eyes: jewels and precious jugs and bowls, his horses and his women. His slaves do his bidding and the scene is one of great violence, but the king is unmoved, even by the almost sexual abandon of the girls (sisters, surely, of Ingres's houris). For all the agitation it is a quiet picture. In spite of the near-chaos of the cornucopian composition, attention focusses on the heavy, immobile and spiritually detached figure of Sardanapalus. Neither he nor the others are drawn with much accuracy—he looks very much like a Henry Moore sculp-

14

2. **Eugène Delacroix.** *Studies for the Death of Sardanapalus. c.* 1827. Pen and wash. 8 × 12⅓ in. (20.5 × 31.4 cm.). Louvre, Paris. As these studies show, Delacroix was more intent on finding dramatic and affecting figures and relationships than naturalistic accuracy.

ture—and if we examine a preparatory drawing for the picture, we can see at once that anatomical accuracy was no part of Delacroix's programme, but rather expressive pose and movement, to which in the painting he added colour and chiaroscuro. The picture is full of musical qualities, with passages that communicate their emotional content long before they are recognised for what they represent, with shapes that stand out like melodies to reappear elsewhere in developed form, and with groupings within the total composition that seem almost like symphonic movements. Delacroix had a passionate love for music, which seemed to him the finest of the arts for its direct appeal to the emotions, and he often spoke of musical qualities in painting. He wrote: 'There is an impression produced by a given arrangement of colour, light, shade, etc.. This is what might be called the music of a picture'. One of the basic themes of nineteenth-century painting is the growing value attached to this pictorial music, and the conflict between this and the representational aspect of painting.

Among these musical qualities in painting, colour is of prime importance. In this respect particularly, Delacroix prepared the ground for many a subsequent painter. He learned much from Veronese, Rubens, Titian and Rembrandt. His contemporary, Constable, taught him how to keep an area of colour alive by breaking it up into small touches of differing shades and tones of that colour. From observation he learned the colour content of shadows and the mutually invigorating effect produced by complementary colours in juxtaposition. He appears to have known of Chevreul's lectures about colour contrasts through a friend's notes. His visit to North Africa in 1832 greatly developed his awareness of colour, and in subsequent paintings, especially in the great murals he did for a chapel in Sainte-Sulpice (1857–60) and elsewhere, he used complementaries to animate his colour harmonies. His comments on colour are noted in his *Journal* (first published 1893–5) but were available long before that through the writings of assistants and theorists; they were of great seminal importance later, especially to the Post-Impressionists.

Neither Ingres nor Delacroix had followers of great significance. Théodore Chassériau has the distinction of

drawing on both masters without diminishing what they stood for. Others popularised the exotic side of their work, building careers on scenes of North African and Near Eastern life that were vaguely thought of as Oriental. But most of their successors turned out work whose banality facilitated public acclaim. It is against the spongy bulwarks of their established art that a handful of impatient artists were to lead their attacks. Only in the field of landscape painting did other French painters help to lay the foundations for what was to follow in the second half of the century, and to this subject we shall return.

Outside France, Neo-Classical painting flourished but briefly, while Neo-Classical sculpture and architecture endured. Nor did any other country produce grandiose Romantic painting comparable with Delacroix's. Apart from landscape painters, who, from the 1790s onwards come in every spiritual size, the most significant painters are strange individual figures that seem to exist outside the art of their age.

GOYA

The Spaniard, Goya, for instance, may seem to have been as public a painter as anybody, for he was principal painter to Charles IV of Spain. Yet the greater part of his work, and certainly his greatest work, is profoundly personal in character—so much so that one is astonished at the recognition with which his abilities met. Francisco de Goya y Lucientes (1746–1828), David's close contemporary, began his career in a world of faltering Rococo and a decaying court. Neo-Classicism was the revolutionary alternative to Rococo, a public and impersonal art of reconstruction. But Goya chose not to offer visions of a nobler world but to record the sickness of his own, and to this purpose developed a graphic and a painting style that derives from Tiepolo, Velasquez and Rembrandt.

He is the first but not the last painter to use his art to mirror the evils of his time, and his time provided him with exceptional evils. It brought to a decadent Spain war, insurrection and reprisals of a savagery quite abnormal until our own century. Fate gave Goya not only genius but also brought him repeated sickness and total deafness from the

3. **Francisco de Goya.** *Disparate de Miedo* (The *Disparate* of Fear). Etching No. 2 of the *Disparates* or *Proverbios*. Date unknown—this etching appeared in posthumous proofs, 1854–63. 9¾ × 13¾ in. (24.5 × 35 cm.). British Museum, London. Goya not only commented on the condition of his world: he gave visual expression to timeless anxieties that had not before been allowed to form art's content.

age of forty-six. Visual communication alone linked the troubled man to the horrors of the outside world. The first fruit of his particular relationship to the world around is the set of etchings, *Los Caprichos*, begun about 1796 and offered for sale in 1799. Here was something quite different from the social commentary of caricaturists who lampooned the protagonists of society and politics for the entertainment of society. Goya's satire is rooted in compassion, is unpartisan, and ultimately expresses an optimistic sense of misery resulting more from institutional forces than from individuals. A well-known plate of the *Caprichos* is that inscribed *El sueño de la razón produce monstruos*. The artist sits, sleeping, while dreadful images crowd about his head: 'The dream of reason brings forth monsters'. The world of Romanticism was aware of man's mental activity below the conscious level of its creative power, and some people toyed with subconscious imagery as an alternative to Gothick contrivance. In Goya's case one feels he would rather not have dreamt. It is a painful world he inhabits, in which recognisable subjects mingle with figures out of witchcraft and ancient symbols of evil. A drawing for the same plate has the inscription, 'A universal language, drawn and etched by Francisco de Goya in the year 1797'; his intensely personal vision, he implies, is the common property of us all. And he is right. He records the collapse of eighteenth-century stability in terms that apply to all periods of social disintegration.

Between 1808 and 1815 Goya worked on his second series of etchings, the *Disasters of War* (not published in full until 1863). Here he was dealing with specific events, which he condensed into often quite simple subjects and presented with great dramatic force. Behind these etchings lies the Spanish tradition of the barely sufficient statement: the naked stage, direct communication across the footlights, the complete lack of sentimentality. His large painting, *The Execution of the Rebels on 3 May, 1808* (1814), is related to the series and shows the same bareness and concision. The

figures are grouped with almost diagrammatic clarity, the landscape setting has a primitive bleakness and merely provides an arena for the action, and the faceless soldiers, blind agents of impersonal power, act as one force against their bunch of prisoners. There is a surprising lack of colour. The dominating grey-greens and ochres suggest the colours of Analytical Cubism, just as the picture as a whole sends one, in search of descendants, via Manet to Picasso's *Guernica*. Goya is clearly in the Baroque tradition, yet the clarity of this design is such that one can compare it with David's in *The Oath of the Horatii*. Not only do Neo-Classicism and Romantic Baroque meet as equals in this picture, but they join hands with the primitive Renaissance art of Giotto as Goya jettisons all the skills of painting trees and landscape and individualised human beings for the sake of his emotional impact.

The anti-naturalistic and fantastic element in Goya's art that frequently showed in his previous work, dominates his next series of etchings, the *Disparates* (Curiosities) or *Los Proverbios*, etched between 1815 and 1820. These, like the paintings he did on the walls of his house during the same years, are all images of profound anxiety. Such work could not produce immediate followers. Indeed, one is tempted to see Goya as the end of a development and a national school. But the *Caprichos* were known in France and England (Delacroix, for example, made drawings after the whole set), and from the 1860s onwards Goya has been recognised as part of our artistic inheritance in that fundamental, inalienable way shared perhaps only by Michelangelo and Rembrandt. All his work radiates his humanity. He is the first great artist to have treated contemporary horrors as his material. In a very un-Baroque and modern way he chose subjects without heroes, in which the protagonists are the anonymous multitude and nothing is achieved but a secular and pointless martyrdom. He is the first and greatest painter of the absurd.

BRITISH PAINTING: BLAKE

In England portraiture still received the lion's share of artists' and patrons' attention. Gainsborough and Reynolds had brought to it exceptional talents, and had promulgated a new kind of portrait, informal even when presenting princes, that had considerable influence on the Continent. But Reynolds condemned the low ambitions of artists content with portrait painting and worked for a situation in which painters and sculptors could emulate the great Italians and devote themselves to treating important historical and religious themes in a classical manner. His pleas had some effect. A small number of influential but not very agreeable British artists (and Americans in Britain) contributed to the development of international Neo-Classicism.

Britain's major nineteenth-century painters did not fit Reynolds' prescription. William Blake (1757–1827) detested everything Reynolds stood for. He wanted passion, imagination, the rejection of everything that smacks of

(Continued on page 33)

4. **William Blake.** *Laocoon.* c. 1818. Line engraving. 15 × 11 in. (38 × 27.5 cm.). Sir Geoffrey Keynes Collection, London. Blake's annotated version of the *Laocoon* group (a Hellenistic sculpture) presents his anti-authoritarian view of art. Rationalism and naturalism are art's enemies; a passionate imagination is art's only true source.

1, 2. **Jacques Louis David.** *The Oath of the Horatii* (above). Oil on canvas. 130 × 168 in. (330 × 427 cm.). Louvre, Paris. *The Sabine Women* (below), 1799. Oil on canvas. 152 × 245 in. (386 × 520 cm.). Louvre, Paris. Two stages in David's Neo-Classicism are represented here: masculine severity in the earlier work succeeded by greater elegance and elaboration in the later. But both paintings use ancient history to comment on the contemporary world, and their function is to uplift and instruct more than to entertain. They thus reject the purely decorative function of Rococo painting.

3. **Jean Auguste Dominique Ingres.**
The Turkish Bath. 1863. Oil on canvas.
$42\frac{1}{2}$ in. (108 cm.) diameter. Louvre,
Paris. Although Ingres considered himself
the champion of the new classicism, his
work often incorporates elements of fantasy and of Baroque design which shows
that Neo-Classicism must be regarded as
one facet of Romanticism. Typical of his
time is Ingres's fascinated interest in the
Near East; exceptional for his time, the
expressiveness of his design and the subservience to it of naturalistic appearances.

4. (opposite). **Théodore Géricault.**
Horse Frightened by Thunder and Lightning.
1920–21. Oil on canvas. $19\frac{1}{4} \times 25\frac{5}{8}$ in.
(49×60 cm.). Reproduced by courtesy
of the Trustees of the National Gallery,
London. Painting and horses were the
twin passions of Géricault's life and he
combined them on several occasions.
But the horse had a special significance
for Romantic art generally as a pure and
noble beast of exceptional sensitivity,
with Arab associations.

5. **Eugène Delacroix.** *The Death of
Sardanapalus.* 1827. Oil on canvas.
145×195 in. (395×495 cm.). Louvre,
Paris. One of the largest and most complex
of Delacroix's easel paintings, *Sardanapalus*
is also one of the most turbulent, embodying the half-guilty regard for Near-Eastern barbaric pleasures of his time.
Delacroix has filled his picture with incident and with dynamic forms and
colours, yet every part is anchored to the
compelling stillness of the king, whose
formal weight resolves the restless jig-saw
puzzle of bodies and objects just as the
white of his robe appears to subsume all
the other colours of the painting.

6. **Francisco de Goya y Lucientes.**
The Execution of the Rebels on 3rd May, 1808.
1814. Oil on canvas. 104½ × 135½ in.
(266 × 345 cm.). Prado, Madrid. The
coincidence of Goya and the Napoleonic
wars in Spain produced a new kind of
painting: on the scale of a history painting,
but using a contemporary subject without
heroes to celebrate. Here there are no
names, no glorification, but a bare, powerful statement of man's pointless inhu-
manity. The whole picture is directed
towards this statement—little colour,
composition and artificial light concen-
trating attention on the action, the execu-
tioners abstracted for the sake of concision
and expression. It is thus a distant forerunner of the bare stage of modern drama.

7. **William Blake.** *The Simoniac Pope.*
c. 1825–27. Watercolour. 14½ × 20½ in.
(37 × 52 cm.). Reproduced by courtesy
of the Trustees of the Tate Gallery,
London. One of an unfinished set of
Dante illustrations done in the last years of
Blake's life. His visionary art is seen here
at its most clarified—the many sources on
which he drew having been integrated
within a personal style that has little con-
nection with the art of Blake's time.

8. **John Constable.** *Barges on the Stour, with Dedham Church. c.* 1811. Oil on paper laid on canvas. 10¼ × 12¼ in. (26 × 31 cm.). Victoria and Albert Museum, London. (Henry Vaughan Bequest).

It is customary nowadays to insist on the vigour and freshness of Constable's exhibition pieces, the larger paintings for which studies such as this oil sketch were done. They lack, however, the fluency of his small sketches, the immediacy of notation and the truth to natural appearances that combine to give the impression of absolute spontaneity and disguise the wealth of artistic skill and scientific knowledge that went into them. Constable's view of the natural world has become so integral a part of ours that it requires an act of will to remember that the reality of his pictures is not nature's reality but art's. 'It is the business of a painter', he wrote in 1824, 'not to contend with nature ... but to make something out of nothing, in attempting which, he must almost of necessity become poetical'.

9, 10. **Joseph Mallord William Turner.**
Norham Castle. c. 1840–45, (above) and
*Snowstorm—Steamboat off a Harbour's
Mouth.* 1841–42, (below). Both oil on
canvas. 36 × 48 in. (91.5 × 122 cm.).
Reproduced by courtesy of the Trustees of
the Tate Gallery, London. In his late work,
Turner's interest in the dramatic situations
offered by history and fiction (so dear to
his age) shifted to the dramatic situations
often provided by nature. Light is the
dominant visible element in land and
seascape, and it becomes a major part of
Turner's concern, so that he seems to offer
a link between Claude in the seventeenth
century, and the French Impressionists
later in the nineteenth. But he also sought
pictorial form and structure through
which to express the energy, the drama or
the sweetness of nature, her serenity or her
turbulence, and this he had to invent and
to assess in terms of its correspondence
with his emotional, as well as visual
experience. In this respect he stands
beside Cézanne in uncovering issues that
still challenge the modern artist.

11. **Gustave Courbet.** *The Studio.* 1855. Oil on canvas. 142 × 235½ in. (361 × 598 cm.). Louvre, Paris. With his country background and his attachment to the realities of the visible world, Courbet saw himself as the champion of Realism (his own term). His themes were from the real world, richly and potently conveyed in paint. Here, however, he combines a realistic manner with a synthetic subject. This statement about the world around him and his own place in it is expressed in dramatised and partly symbolical terms. The section on the right includes portraits of some of his friends: on the extreme right the poet and art critic, Baudelaire.

12. (left). **Théodore Rousseau.** *The Plain of Montmartre. c.* 1835. Oil on panel. 92¾ × 139¾ in. (235 × 355 cm.). Louvre, Paris. In the 1830s, Rousseau came to be recognised as the champion of anti-academic landscape painting among that liberal-minded part of Paris's art public that also admired Delacroix. This, and his disregard of the classical qualities through which, according to academic opinion, landscape could be raised to the level of art, meant repeated rejection by the jury of the *Salon*. His work became more tranquil in the 1840s and subsequently received some recognition, which turned to fame and popularity in the 70s—by which time the Impressionists were bearing the brunt of conventional disapproval. Rousseau owed much to Claude and to the Dutch school of the seventeenth century, but he was instinctively drawn to open-air painting of landscape, and English painters, particularly Constable, had an important effect on him. In his work of the 1830s Rousseau adds to such influences an emotional quality that is Byronic rather than (as in the case of Constable) Wordsworthian.

13. **Jean François Millet.** *The Woodsawyers. c.* 1850–52. Oil on canvas. 22½ × 32 in. (57 × 81 cm.). Victoria and Albert Museum, London. (Ionides Bequest). Millet, after ten years in Paris, abandoned city life for a rustic environment and painted pictures in which the life of peasants is given symbolical status. He was much influenced by earlier Dutch painters. Van Gogh greatly admired his work, and painted several versions of some of Millet's compositions.

14. **Jean Baptiste Camille Corot.** *Ville d'Avray. c.* 1835–38. Oil on canvas. 11 × 16 in. (28 × 40 cm.). Louvre, Paris. Dutch influence and the open-air painting of landscape were transformed in the art of Corot by his deep sense of classical structure. Thus he can be seen as a milestone on the road from Poussin, in the seventeenth century, to Cézanne, just as his regard for the transient sense impressions offered by the constantly changing face of nature makes him a forerunner of the Impressionists. The moderate fame he achieved during his lifetime was largely on account of the more 'finished' and anecdotal studio compositions he sent to the *Salon. Ville d'Avray* is one of his small outdoor paintings, an outstanding example of his ability to reconcile freshness of vision with a composition which is almost geometric in structure.

15. **Caspar David Friedrich.** *The Cross
and the Cathedral in the Mountains. c.* 1811.
Oil on canvas. 17¾ × 15 in. (45 × 38 cm.).
Kunstmuseum, Düsseldorf. A North
German with an essentially mystical
conception of nature, Friedrich painted
melancholy portraits of particular
stretches of landscape as well as visionary
scenes in which landscape is combined
with symbolical matter. In this small
picture the visionary is to the fore,
although the rocks and branches of the
lower portion reveal his close study of
natural appearances. The hieratic sym-
metry of the Crucifix, the church and the
trees gives a supernatural quality to the
scene which is rendered disquieting by the
complete absence of man—as though
Divinity had deposited that integrated
artifact on the irregular surface of the
earth.

16. **Peter von Cornelius.** *Joseph Revealing
Himself to his Brothers.* 1816. Fresco
painting. 93 × 114¼ in. (236 × 290 cm.).
Nationalgalerie, East Berlin. In drawing
unashamedly on Central Italian painting
of around 1500, the Nazarenes challenged
the long-established right of artists to base
themselves on the art of Raphael and his
successors, and drew attention to the
virtues of a more two-dimensional, more
brightly coloured and less grandiloquent
art. Cornelius was the most intelligent and
self-critical of the group. This fresco is one
of a series he painted for the Prussian
Consul-General in Rome.

17. **Auguste Rodin.** *Head of Grief.* Before 1882. Bronze. 9¼ in. high. (23.5 cm.). Musée Rodin, Paris. The expression of extreme anguish in this work is comparable, through the history of art, to such sculptures as the Hellenistic *Laocoon* and the dying Christs and martyrs, achieved through a mixture of realism and expressionism.

19. **Adolf Friedrich von Menzel.** *The Artist's Sister with a Candle.* 1847. Oil on canvas. 18 × 12½ in. (46 × 32 cm.). Bayerische Staatsgemäldesammlungen, Munich. Menzel was admired for his historical scenes celebrating with cinematic verve the eighteenth-century Court of Frederick the Great. But he also painted a series of very personal pictures (mostly in the 1840s) that reveal his extraordinary gifts as an observer of light and atmosphere in simple domestic scenes.

18. **William Holman Hunt.** *The Hireling Shepherd.* 1851. Oil on canvas. 30 × 42½ in. (76 × 103 cm.). Reproduced by courtesy of the City Art Gallery, Manchester. Moralising content combined with an essentially moral sense of truth to appearances, makes the work of the Pre-Raphaelites at once characteristic of mid-Victorian bourgeois values, yet revolutionary in the brightness of tones and colours and the democratic evenness of attention given to all parts of the canvas.

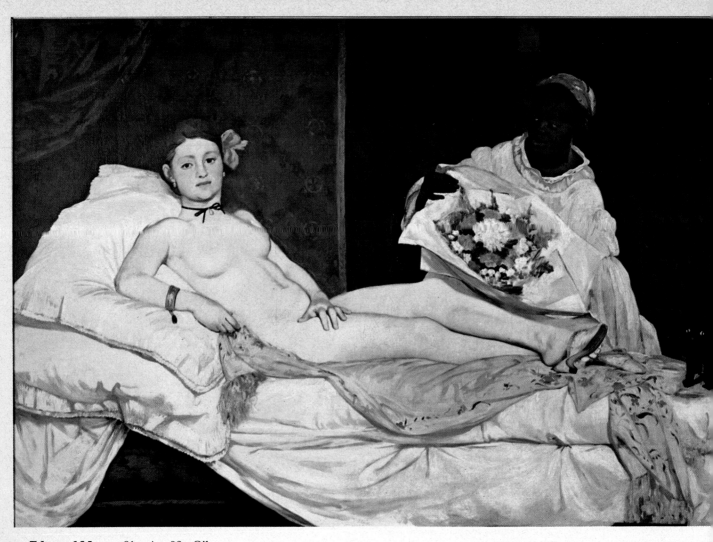

20. **Edouard Manet.** *Olympia*. 1863. Oil on canvas. 51¼ × 74¾ in. (130 × 190 cm.). Musée de l'Impressionnisme, Paris. One of the most controversial paintings in the history of art, *Olympia* was still a matter for violent disagreement when it was accepted by the Louvre in 1907. Manet was clearly linking himself to the long tradition of the female nude in art, particularly in Venetian painting, but it seemed to his contemporaries that he was mocking that tradition by denying its erotic function. He arranged his subject so that its three-dimensionality was minimal, and gave the flowers and the draperies an attractiveness he did not allow the girl's head and body. However, she is painted in not so very different a way from Ingres's subtly under-modelled nudes.

21. **Kitagawa Utamaro.** *Child Upsetting a Goldfish Bowl*. 1755–1806. Wood-block print on paper. 15¼ × 9⅞ in. (38.75 × 25 cm.). Department of Oriental Antiquities, British Museum, London. Japanese prints exerted a great influence on the painters in Paris in the 1860s who were turning away from the elaborate three-dimensionality achieved by perspective and tonal modelling. These prints offered pictorial harmony and rhythms of an entirely unnaturalistic kind.

5. **Henry Fuseli.** *Macbeth and the Armed Head. c.* 1770–78. Pen, ink, sepia, and grey wash. 14⅞ × 10⅛ in. (37.75 × 25.7 cm.). Width uneven. British Museum, London. Fuseli's admiration for sixteenth-century Italian art, as well as his highly developed sense of the dramatic, shows especially clearly in his visualisation of scenes from Shakespeare and from Milton.

moderation and good breeding. 'The road of excess', he wrote, 'leads to the palace of wisdom'. In his poetry and his art, often in combination, he presented a view of the world in which man, through his mental and physical powers and desires, is directly linked to the supernatural. ' "What," it will be Question'd, "When the Sun rises, do you not see a round disk of fire somewhat like a Guinea?" O no, no, I see an Innumerable company of the Heavenly host crying, "Holy, Holy is the Lord God Almighty".' He took pictorial ideas from a wide range of sources—from contemporaries, from Greek and medieval art, from Italian Mannerism, and above all from Michelangelo—and he used a variety of often original techniques, but the chief thing that separates him from all his contemporaries in his almost exclusive concern with the world of the spirit at a time when art rarely dealt with anything beyond the physical horizon. His poetry and his art are entirely visionary; sometimes he claimed to be working on the instructions of supernatural agents. What he searched for aesthetically was clarity and vigour, and at times a fluency of design that later make him seem a forerunner of Art Nouveau. Line was his chief means of expression; colour was secondary. Chiaroscuro and academic modelling he rejected as destructive of clarity. Because of this, it would be tempting to hail him as a precursor of Impressionism but of course he did not concern himself with light any more than with other aspects of naturalism. All his pictures embody complex literary ideas, often his own, and it must be remembered that he should be seen as an illustrator rather than a painter in the usual sense, working in a field where conventional pressure was lighter, even if the seriousness and originality of his art makes him one of the greatest figures of his time.

THE RISE OF LANDSCAPE PAINTING

The most important achievement of British art in the first half of the nineteenth century certainly lies in landscape painting. Indeed, the dramatic rise of landscape painting generally in this period is the most significant event in nineteenth-century European art. It is not surprising that the era in which the effects of the industrial revolution be-

came visible, in which towns grew and darkened as peasants were turned into the proletariat, should also have seen a new and compensating love of landscape. But the deep sense of landscape as divinity revealed, already expressed in James Thomson's widely translated poem *The Seasons* (1726) and spread, as we have seen, by Rousseau and others, is an essential part of the new appreciation of wild nature. The resistance to landscape painting was considerable. Academic theory saw little value in it, and next to none when pictures represented particular stretches of country void of classical associations. For artists exploring this new field, a sense of moral significance was a necessary support—their only historical support came from the Dutch school of the seventeenth century, and none at all from the generally admired masters of the Renaissance. The opposition must have realised that landscape painting, if it was accepted as serious art, would make a breach in the academic concept of art as a language addressed principally to the mind. A landscape by Constable needs to be read in a different way from David's *Oath of the Horatii*. The latter presumes a knowledge of ancient history, the ability to recognise the story's relevance to his time, and a willingness to accept one moment of the story as standing for the whole; its full appreciation requires some knowledge of classical design. Constable's landscape demands a response not from the intellect but from the affections; the most common human experience of nature will go a long way towards meeting his demands, though a familiarity with the countryside and a devotion to it similar to his own would help one further. That this kind of art should become, during the later part of the century, the pace-maker of European painting suggests, first, a shift of interest from an art with a specific content to an art of generalised and indefinable meaning, and, second, a profound change of attitude in the beholder. The landscape painting demands of the spectator that he project himself into it. Far from involving a dehumanisation of art through the demotion, or even the dismissal of man as the visible subject, it opened the doors of appreciation to a far wider body of spectators and implied a descent of art from its pedestal of privilege and scholarship. This meant a new and almost exclusive emphasis by the painter on the unliterary elements in his art. It allowed him a freedom from realism and from specific representation that could not then have been achieved in an art dependent on the figure and on narrative. In short, landscape painting was the ideal art for the full exploitation of those aspects of painting that Delacroix called 'musical'.

LANDSCAPE PAINTING IN BRITAIN:
CONSTABLE AND TURNER

In the first half of the nineteenth century it is certainly England that plays the leading role in this development. The nature poetry of Wordsworth coincides in time with the emergence of the new landscape painting. Blake himself gave it some impetus through his primitive little woodcuts illustrating *The Pastorals of Virgil* (published 1821); indeed, his immediate influence is more apparent in landscapists such as Samuel Palmer than in figure painting. More immediately relevant is the pioneering work of Richard Wilson and Thomas Gainsborough who in the eighteenth century attempted to find English paraphrases for, respectively, the Roman scenes of Claude and the Dutch portrait-landscapes of Ruisdael and Hobbema. These and other precursors of English Romantic landscape painting, helped to educate some part of the public towards a taste for landscape and eased the Academy's acceptance of such work. Constable and Turner never had to face the rigorous official displeasure that landscape painters in France encountered.

One is tempted to contrast Constable and Turner as the country boy who gave his life to expressing an innocent attachment to the environment of his youth, and the town boy who discovered nature as a strange and partly inimical 8 force. Certainly John Constable (1776–1837), who never ceased to feel a special relationship to his native Suffolk, and in his choice of subjects from other counties seldom stirred from scenes of comparable peace and simplicity, came as near as we can imagine feasible to recording normal, rather than exceptional appearances. That he should have had the firmness of purpose to persevere with this at a time when the representation of landscape was still beset by weighty conventions of composition, colour, tone and subject, gives him the character of a rebel. This does not mean that he did not evolve conventions of his own and borrow from earlier landscape painters (particularly the Dutch and Rubens), especially in producing the six-foot canvases that he considered his most important works. Behind them lie pencil and oil sketches whose extraordinary degree of naturalism was the result of years of painstaking observation of nature under varying conditions of season and weather. In his time the science we know as meteorology was being born, and he himself considered landscape painting 'a branch of natural philosophy', that is, physics, but of greater underlying importance was his sense that moral feeling should be the content of his art. Constable was an instinctively religious man. 'Everything seems full of blossom of some kind, and at every step I take, and on whatever object I turn my eyes, that sublime expression of the Scriptures: "I am the resurrection and the life", seems as if uttered near me.' To him, as to Wordsworth whom he often quoted, closeness to nature was closeness to God. The sky, he said, was in all landscape painting 'the chief organ of sentiment', and it was the sky particularly that he studied with the attention that others gave to figure drawing. Because of his skies and the freshness of his tones, Constable is spoken of as a forerunner of Impressionism, yet he was too much the Northerner, too much involved in the physical character of the objects he brought together in his paintings ('willows, old rotten planks, slimy posts, and brickwork, I love such things'), to allow light to dominate over all. But he did demonstrate the aesthetic significance of unexceptional motifs, and he painted them with a vividness and a technical freedom that was to influence painters in France and Germany.

While Constable's art is essentially English—not merely for the subjects he chose, but equally for the Wordsworthian sentiments—Turner's is European or even global. He begins by testing himself against all kinds of predecessors: Wilson, the Dutch marine painters and landscapists (including Rembrandt), Canaletto and Guardi, Poussin and Claude, Gainsborough and the Norwich watercolourists. In his own watercolours he is more detached, more personal; one senses an Oriental delicacy and understatement that may have been inspired by Chinese art. Then he specialises. The character in any work that enables us to recognise its author is a product of specialisation, and a focussing of interest to the exclusion of other possibilities. Turner—and this is a remarkably modern characteristic—specialises to the point where his art becomes incomprehensible to his contemporaries. Quite early on heads are shaken. Benjamin West, President of the Royal Academy, said in 1805 that Turner's works were 'tending to imbecility'; Hazlitt in 1816 quoted an anonymous wit as saying that they were 'pictures of nothing and very like'. Later even Turner's admirers had to agree that his art had gone astray.

J. M. W. Turner (1775–1851), the precocious son of a London barber, was more blatantly a Romantic painter than Constable. From his early days he knew the value of simple, self-contained motifs, but there was in him a drive to the elemental and the heroic that led him into more rhetorical subject-matter. *The Battle of the Nile*, selected *Plagues of Egypt*, *The army of the Medes destroyed in the desert by a whirlwind*, *The Deluge*, *The Destruction of Sodom*—such subjects offered him opportunities for Wagnerian presentations in which dramatic narrative is partnered by equally dramatic staging. Later the staging was to dominate. When 9 in Yorkshire Turner experienced a particularly fine thunderstorm, he jotted down notes of its forms and colours on the back of a letter and told his companion, 'Hawkey; in two years you will see this again, and call it *Hannibal crossing the Alps*'. And so it was (1812). Between 1830 and his death, he painted pictures whose shared subject is the energy

6. **Honoré Daumier.** *Battle of the Schools: Classic Idealism v. Realism*, from *Charivari*, 24th April, 1855. Lithograph. 10¼ × 8¼ in. (27 × 21 cm.). Bibliothèque Nationale, Paris. Daumier's cartoon opposes a muscular and ruffianly painter to a frail and bespectacled version of David's Romulus in *The Sabine Women*.

of nature, or rather the vortices of brushstroke and the colour and weight of paint in which such a theme can be communicated. They look essentially visionary, and in a way they are. At an advanced age Turner had himself lashed to the mast of boat in a storm, and then he painted a picture 'to show what such a scene was like': *Snow Storm— steamboat off a harbour's mouth* (1842), but one hesitates to accept the picture as a bare record, just as one hesitates to accept Turner's action as mere fact-finding. What Turner sought was a visible equivalent for a complex of sensations that were not exclusively visual, and this equivalent, to be a picture, had to have an imposed coherence. Small wonder that his contemporaries did not know what to make of such work: it looks beyond Impressionism to Expressionism in its vehemence and technical freedom, and to Futurism in its intentions.

This technical freedom was the product of innate brilliance (Turner was made a full member of the Royal Academy in 1802, at the age of twenty-seven), years of experimentation and study, and ultimately the rejection of skills he no longer needed. Long before Cézanne, Turner brought watercolour methods into his handling of oils, and was attacked for it. He studied colour, in Goethe's theory and in his own and the old masters' practice, with a thoroughness that even Delacroix could not match; colour and what the Futurists in 1910 were to call *linee-forze* (strictly 'line forces') became the visible constituents of his art. If this makes him sound like an abstract artist, no matter; Turner appears to have been the first painter to have had a picture hung upside down and to have said they should leave it, it looked better that way.

LANDSCAPE PAINTING IN FRANCE

Constable and Turner were certainly the outstanding landscape painters of their age, but the rise of landscape was a European phenomenon. In France the Barbizon School produced paintings with something of Constable's closeness to nature and poetic feeling. Théodore Rousseau

(1812–1867) was particularly affected by the example of England. He and Jean François Millet (1814–1875) lived almost continuously in the village of Barbizon on the edge of the Forest of Fontainebleau, painting the land and the rustic life around them. Others spent periods working with them, like Charles François Daubigny (1817–1878), probably the first artist to complete his paintings out of doors. Attractive and comforting as these painters' works appear to us now, it is difficult to understand why French officialdom should have so denigrated and feared them. But the French had no tradition of naturalism and suspected the Barbizon painters, with their untrimmed beards, of being political revolutionaries as well as underminers of classical values. Even J. B. C. Corot (1796–1875), who was willing to turn his luminous landscape sketches into relatively conventional classical landscapes for exhibition at the *Salon*, had difficulty in having his work accepted. His smaller, more personal, pictures combine simple organisation with a justness of tone that is almost the equal of Constable's (some of whose works he had seen and admired).

COURBET AND DAUMIER

Realism of one kind or another, however, became the dominant mode of French painting in the middle years. Much of this was of the laboured story-telling kind that long continued to enjoy the unwearing and uninformed support of the middle classes and were painted by men who, were they living today, might be producing second-rate films. Gustave Courbet (1819–1877) earned the hatred of the art public of his time with a realism that went beyond the bounds of good manners. His anti-intellectualism and anti-clericalism, his unsentimental view of such a privileged subject as the female figure, his passion for the physical presence and his belief that anything other than that was an evasion of truth, made him the most attacked artist of his time. His finest works tend to be his landscapes but his range was wide and included still-life, nudes, a monumental portrayal of a *Burial at Ornans* (1850)—a scene of peasant life presented with the grandiloquence David brought to Napoleon's crowning of his wife—and a number of large pictures celebrating the greatness and humanity of Courbet. *The Studio* (1855) synthesises his interests. On one side of the large picture there are peasants, poachers and beggars; on the other side a few of his friends. In the middle, between an admiring child and a nude model whose presence in the crowded studio was an affront to decency, sits the painter himself, finishing a landscape with a few fine, operatic gestures.

Honoré Daumier (1808–1879) was a realist of another kind. A glazier's son, he grew up in Paris. He learned the craft of lithography and in 1831 began to work for the journal *La Caricature*. In 1832 he was imprisoned for one of his political cartoons, but returned to work after six months in gaol. In 1834 *La Caricature* was suppressed; from then on Daumier worked for *Charivari*. More or less untrained, he had turned himself into one of the great draughtsmen of western art. To his extraordinary fluency and power of drawing he joined a deep sense of social injustice and a personal understanding of urban poverty and pretensions. His political attacks could not have been so bitter had not his kinship with the masses been so close. His lithographs were admired by well-known artists, such as Corot and Delacroix. The novelist, Balzac, who also worked for *Charivari*, said of him: 'This boy has something of Michelangelo under his skin'. Scarcely anyone was aware that he was also a remarkable painter, using paints with a freedom unknown to his contemporaries.

GERMAN ROMANTIC PAINTING

Germany, too, in the first decades of the century produced notable landscape painters. These owed more to the traditions of Baroque landscape and to late eighteenth-century pioneers such as J. P. Hackert and J. C. Brand than to British or French example which contributed more in the middle and later years of the century. The most original figure among them was Caspar David Friedrich (1774–1840). He was born on the Baltic coast and studied at the Copenhagen Academy, but he lived most of his life in Dresden painting landscapes in which his intimacy with all parts of Germany provided him with the means to express strong Romantic sensations of cosmic anguish. He exploited the thrilling forms of Gothic ruins and Alpine peaks. He employed great vistas of open land and seascape and placed in them minute and solitary figures. After Friedrich's death his work was quickly forgotten. Its Nordic qualities appealed less to his successors than the Romantic realism of the Barbizon School. One of his friends was Philipp Otto Runge (1777–1810), remembered outside Germany more for his treatise on colour, published in 1810, than for his elaborate paintings in which a detailed and factual manner, sometimes uplifted by his almost religious valuation of light, is combined with mystical and symbolical content. At a less intense level, similar qualities can be found in the work of the Nazarenes, a group of artists that was formed in Vienna

and moved to Rome in 1809. They devoted themselves to the propagation of painting in the manner of the *quattrocento* Italians with elements introduced from German art of the age of Dürer. They wanted to find in Christian art a simplicity and energy that the Neo-Classicist had found in paganism. Their most important contribution to the art of the century was the attention they paid to mural painting.

THE BRITISH PRE-RAPHAELITE BROTHERHOOD

In Britain, the revolutionary atmosphere of the middle of the century threw up a group of painters whose aims were in some respects similar to those of the Nazarenes. The Pre-Raphaelite Brotherhood was formed in 1848 by three young painters, William Holman Hunt (1827–1910), John Everett Millais (1829–96) and Dante Gabriel Rossetti (1828–82), in protest against the polite untruths of academic painting. They demanded an art full of meaning, presented with absolute accuracy. Their works were much ridiculed when they began, and they have frequently been ridiculed since, but their passionate attachment to detailed appearance, including its colour, their use of white grounds and very pure paints to capture and hold this colour, their insistence on clear narrative through clear design—these aspects of their work made them not only revolutionary within the British art world of their time but also influential in the last years of the century, during the rise of Art Nouveau.

ASPECTS OF REALISM

So the Pre-Raphaelites, too, were realists of a kind, and realism seems to have been a common denominator of European art once the more subjective phases of Romanticism had passed their climax. Any continuing commitment to realism, however, soon confronts the painter with insuperable difficulties. In developing a convincing pictorial language to express the three-dimensional and mobile world in which he lives, the realist painter has to decide which kind of falsification best fits his purpose. Constable had dealt brilliantly with aspects of reality particularly far removed from the reality of paints and canvas, especially with regard to light and intimations of growth and change. He and others had proved the value of a non-academic technique as a means to vitality. Today we find the small oil sketches of Constable, Corot and others more naturalistic than their larger, exhibitable works, but in their own time it was the other way round. Sketchy techniques were systematised around 1870 by the Impressionists into a new style of painting and ultimately led to idioms far removed from naturalism. The establishment of loose configurations of brushstrokes as a legible and serious means of painting and as an alternative, to say the least, to the laboured finish admired in the academies, is one of the major achievements of early nineteenth-century painting.

SCULPTURE IN THE AGE OF ROMANTICISM

What, one wonders, would have happened to painting if

archaeological search had thrown up as vast a quantity of classical painting as it did of sculpture and architecture? The pressure of antiquity on sculpture, through these discoveries, through the writings of such men as Winckelmann, and for lack of any thriving sculptural tradition, was enough to take almost all life out of the art. The Italian, Antonio Canova (1757–1822), was the leading Neo-Classical sculptor in Europe. An able and likeable person as well as a strict upholder of classical ideals, Canova with his assistants was responsible for a great quantity of what Hildebrandt later described as 'petrified human bodies'. Countless others followed his example, pre-eminently the Dane, Bertel Thorwaldsen. It is no exaggeration to say that, in a century when the other arts worked from constantly altering premises, the Neo-Classical sculptors appointed themselves guardians of the Greco-Roman tradition, not to say of European civilisation. Their successors continued to hold this pose for the rest of the century. This does not mean that all these sculptors were inept or unprincipled. The opposite would be truer: many of the men who gave their lives to creating variations on classical prototypes were paragons of sincerity and diligence. Some of them, indeed, were men with more than a touch of genius, like the Englishman, John Flaxman (1755–1826), the friend of Blake, whose sculpture has a freedom unknown in Continental Neo-Classicism, and whose long series of cool line illustrations to Homer, Hesiod, Dante and others, shaped the international taste of his time.

The only sign of any liberalising activity within the sculpture of this period comes from the few sculptors who tried to oppose a relative realism to the idealism of the classicists. While this meant some loosening of classical conventions, it could not at this time mean much more than a move towards the Baroque. Even this degree of deviation was more or less limited to France, where Delacroix could offer support and example. François Rude (1784–1855)

7. **Antonio Canova.** *Stuart Monument.* 1819. Marble sculpture in St Peter's, Rome. Skilled, efficient and likeable, Canova triumphantly rode the wave of Neo-Classicism and by his success played a great part in burdening his successors with the weight of the classical tradition.

8. **John Flaxman.** *Orestes Pursued by the Furies.* From *Compositions from the Tragedies of Aeschylus* designed by John Flaxman, engraved by Thomas Piroli. 1793. 12 × 7 in. (30.5 × 17.8 cm.). Reproduced from 'Flaxman's Classical Outlines', 1874. A fine Neo-Classical sculptor with an unexpected penchant for Gothic art, Flaxman was most important in his time for his line illustrations, which were studied all over Europe and guided painters and sculptors towards a feeling for the incisive quality of classical forms.

9. **François Rude.** *Departure of Volunteers.*
1836. Stone. On the east façade of the Arc
de Triomphe, Paris. Like Delacroix, and
possibly under his influence, Rude opposed Baroque richness and complexity
to the Neo-Classicism of his time.

10. **Antoine-Louis Barye.** *Jaguar Devour-
ing a Crocodile. c.* 1850–55. Bronze. $3\frac{1}{4} \times 9\frac{1}{2}$
in. (8×24 cm.). Ny Carlsberg Glypothek,
Copenhagen. Barye's vigorous sculptures
of animals were not acceptable to the
Salon, which upheld the Greek tradition
of idealised human beauty.

11. **Honoré Daumier.** *Jacques Lefèbre. 'L'esprit fin et tranchant.'* 1830–2. Coloured clay. 8. in. high (20 cm.). Musée des Beaux-Arts, Marseilles. Daumier made his satirical busts of French parliamentarians as models for his political caricatures. It is possible that the soft medium of clay helped him to achieve that expressive exaggeration of selected features that is the essence of caricature.

9 made his relief on the Arc de l'Etoile a few years after Delacroix painted his *Liberty on the Barricades*. Antoine Louis Barye (1796–1875) long studied the forms and movements 10 of animals in the Paris *Jardins des Plantes*, but his animal sculptures, for all their basis in observation, are shot through with a Baroque and Romantic sense of action and energy that takes very similar forms in the paintings of Rubens and Delacroix. To inject this energy into sculpture is a considerable achievement. Undoubtedly Barye's concentration of animal subjects gave him a freedom he could hardly have exercised in figure sculpture; at the same time it should be noted that work of this kind meant repeated exclusion from the *Salon*.

In this situation the sculpture of Daumier comes as a 11 complete surprise, particularly the small busts of politicians he made in the 1830s. They were his means of finding that exaggerated yet unmistakable version of his subjects that is the essence of caricature. He had no sculptural training or ambitions; he was free from the limitations of a professional sculptor working for a public and in a tradition. Yet these busts too can be seen as part of a tradition: they belong both to the history of caricature and to the involvement of art in the eighteenth-century pseudoscience of physiognomy, as in the heads sculpted by the German, Messerschmidt, around 1780. But Daumier's busts exist totally outside the art world of his own time.

The weight of classicism apart, there may be other reasons why sculpture at this period is so inferior to painting. Literature was undoubtedly the dominant art form of the age. Although pioneering artists looked to music as their ideal, the arts in general were deeply involved with literature and were judged largely for their literary qualities. Here sculpture is certainly at a disadvantage; it is not a medium suited to narrative. Even so succinct a situation as that presented in *The Oath of the Horatii* could scarcely be treated as statuary. Yet musical qualities were even more out of reach of an art long concerned almost exclusively with the human body. Moreover, for the preceding four centuries sculpture had been losing the primacy it held in ancient and medieval times to painting, and painting had taken over many of sculpture's special functions and characteristics. Sculpture did not attract the greatest talents, and if it did attract a great deal of public patronage, this was often misguided enough to do more harm than good. Even fewer people could appreciate the merits of sculpture than those of painting, and this continues to be true in our own century. The totally unreal world of painting appears to be more open to the kind of dialogue between work and spectator that leads to appreciation than is the physically real yet spiritually unreal world of sculpture. We can go further. The cost of making sculpture, and especially of making it exhibitable, as for example by casting it in bronze, is far greater than that of painting pictures, so that the rebellious sculptor is likely to find himself unable to work at all. The successful sculptor of the nineteenth century, on the other hand, much bespoken for his monuments of generals and civic worthies, his portrait busts and his elaborate tomb sculptures, was likely to gather a team of assistants around him and to arm himself for all the mechanical devices that his century could devise for turning a little clay sketch into a large marble or bronze.

ARCHITECTURE: THE MULTIPLICITY OF STYLES

Much of this applies also to the period's architecture. Here it was not merely the weight of classicism that counted, but rather the bewildering variety of architectural languages that archaeologists and travellers found and described. Architecture had its 'museum without walls' long before painting and sculpture. Each proffered style had its burden of associations and it was these that endeared it to the literary-minded public. In other words, the nineteenth-century patron commissioned buildings on the same partly playful principles as the eighteenth-century aristocrat who required Gothic ruins, Greek temples and Japanese bridges to ornament his grounds. The eighteenth-century patron

12. **Etienne-Louis Boullée.** *Newton Cenotaph.* 1784. Projects of this kind, produced in large quantity during the years of the French Revolution, express the age's hopes of a heroic new world as well as the designer's inclination to bold and affecting forms. The Russian Revolution, too, evoked projects of a semi-visionary kind.

knew a great deal about classical architecture and often provided his own designs. The nineteenth-century merchant or industrialist knew that Gothic architecture spoke of faith and a national past, that Greek architecture suggested a heroic democracy, that Florentine Renaissance architecture celebrated the power of commerce, while more exotic styles (as in the paintings of Ingres, Delacroix and many others) hinted at exotic delights as well as the more calculable values of empire.

NEO-CLASSICAL ARCHITECTURE

This multiplicity of styles presented the designer with opportunities and problems that were unprecedented. The bolder architect at first seized the freedom implied in this multiplicity, so that within the realm of Neo-Classicism we find both the pedantic purveyor of archaeologically accurate replicas of ancient architecture and the inventive designer using the old idiom to subjective and Romantic ends. On paper this could be done with especial virtuosity. The French Revolution threw up a generation of designers for whom classical design, with occasional elements from the Middle Ages, was a starting point for marvellously fanciful inventions. Ledoux and Boullée were the greatest

of them. Etienne Louis Boullée headed his writings on architecture with the motto *Ed io anche son Pittore* ('I too am a painter'), demanding for himself a painter's freedom. His grandiose design for a Newton Cenotaph (1784), a cross 12 between the ancient Mausoleum at Halicarnassus and the Roman Pantheon, suggests a planetarium on a fantastic scale and thus refers to Newton's investigations. Its form is nakedly geometrical, but Boullée's drawing wraps his building in awesome light and shade. Such a design can hardly have been intended for execution. On a more realistic scale, however, the English architect, Sir John Soane (1753–1837), was equally bold. His work for the Bank of England is only one example from a career studded 14 with works of great originality and refinement. The offices he built for the Bank are top-lit, which suited his feeling for dramatic lighting and allowed him to apply his sensitivity for geometrical forms and smooth surfaces to the problem of vaulting. Fundamentally classical in idiom, these offices suggest also the floating domes of Byzantine architecture; their severity is more in accord with Winckelmann's assessment of the Greek spirit than with ancient buildings. Yet there exists a watercolour by Soane showing one of the offices as a ruin in a deserted landscape, standing in some

14. **Sir John Soane.** *Bank of England, the 5% Office, London,* from 1788. Watercolour (by one of Soane's draughtsmen, *c.* 1819). 38 × 28 in. (96.5 × 71 cm.). Soane Museum, London. Soane brought to the classical tradition a rare sensitivity to the poetic qualities of architectural form, nurtured by his interest in non-classical, as well as classical, phases of design. Neo-Classicism was not for him an occasion for subservience to particular Greek or Roman models, but rather an invitation to find a personal and modern equivalent for the strength and simplicity he surmised in the ancients.

13. **Karl Friedrich von Schinkel.** *Altes Museum, Berlin.* 1823–5. Not only is Schinkel's Museum an outstanding example of Neo-Classical design; as a museum it is a building of a new kind, symbolical of the historicism of nineteenth-century European culture.

distant age, with plants sprouting from cracks in the masonry. That so apparently cool and intellectual an architect as Soane should dream of his work in terms of the passing of civilisations under the timeless eye of nature, illuminates the Romantic strain within Neo-Classicism: the Neo-Classicist was aware of the classical past as something distant, destroyed and awesome, and felt for it not the admiring kinship the Renaissance felt for a time when beauty and reason had been brought into unison, but rather the nostalgia a man may feel for his birthplace and a European may feel for the cradle of his civilisation. In more or less overt forms such feelings are expressed in Neo-Classicism everywhere. Comparable in creativeness with Soane was the Berlin architect, Karl Friedrich von Schinkel *13* (1781–1841), first a designer of stage sets and then Prussian State architect. The clarity of his personal classicism lends his buildings an air of exceptional rationality, and there are times when the bareness and near-functionalism of his designs link them to buildings designed a hundred years later, but his logic and his strength is one of visual effectiveness rather than abstract principle—which he could at times apply equally well to buildings in the Gothic style.

PICTURESQUE DESIGN

Visual effectiveness as a criterion for architectural design is a more revolutionary concept than it may seem. It was always one part of a designer's intentions but during the

15. **John Nash.** *Royal Pavilion, Brighton.* Rebuilt and elaborated,
1815. The Prince Regent's pleasure palace by the sea is an
extreme instance of the early nineteenth century's consciousness
of style as an optional ornament. Here a fundamentally classical
building is draped in a fancy dress of Indian and partly
Chinese origin.

Renaissance it had come to be bound up with generally
agreed conventions of rightness whose observance gave intellectual satisfaction as much as optical pleasure. During
the Baroque period there was a greater appeal to the sensations, and it is no surprise to find Baroque architecture,
so much attacked in the eighteenth century, so much admired in the nineteenth. The theoretical bases that had
linked beauty to laws—such as the theory of proportions—
were destroyed in the eighteenth century.

By 1800, the appreciation of architecture rested on the
twin functions of association and sensual effect. Not being a
figurative art, architecture had the advantage of sculpture:
it could approach the condition of music through its qualities of size, mass, space, colour, texture, etc. English design,
as well as English thought, played a leading part in this
development. In the English landscape garden the eighteenth century had evolved an art form dominated by these
two functions, and in the 1760s and 1770s it was widely
imitated on the Continent. The principle of what became
known as the picturesque had already been transferred
from gardens to architecture in Horace Walpole's house,
Strawberry Hill (begun 1748), and by 1800 it was affecting
town planning. In his development of Marylebone Park
(later Regent's Park) and of Regent Street in London
(1811 and after), the architect, John Nash (1752–1835), was
guided entirely by visual effectiveness, swinging Regent
Street in a dramatic curve, hingeing two unaligned streets
on the circular portico of a church, and dropping buildings
like classical back-drops around the landscaped park.
Much the same sense of presentation informed his earlier
work on the Royal Pavilion in Brighton (from 1815 on), a
basically Georgian building which Nash transformed into
a pleasure palace compounded of Indian, Gothic and
Chinese elements. This kind of architecture, though not
necessarily at Nash's level of fantasy or the Prince Regent's
level of expenditure, flourished throughout the greater part
of the century to wrap its patrons in a variety of unreal
environments that compensated for their despoliation of
the real world.

THE SEPARATE WORLD OF ENGINEERING

The men who commissioned Gothic castles, Tuscan villas
and Greek town houses also, directly or indirectly, brought
into town life an unprecedented squalor. The most significant invention of the nineteenth century is the slum. It was
presumably his aversion from the world in which he made
his money that caused the industrialist to draw such a firm
line between his economic and his cultural life. The engineering structures that figure so magnificently on the credit
side of the industrial balance sheet of this time have no
influence on the genteel and protected realm of architecture. The great technical inventions of men like Brunel and

16. **Sir Charles Barry** and **A. W. N. Pugin.** *Houses of Parliament, London.* Designed 1836; built 1840–65. The rebuilding of the British Houses of Parliament was an occasion for debate on the question of an appropriate style. A more or less Tudor style was chosen on the grounds of national pride for a kind of building that had hitherto been linked to Greek democracy via Neo-Classicism.

Telford were of little interest to professional architects intent on recreating the achievements of other ages and civilisations.

STYLES AND MORALITY

In this department life gradually became more earnest. Some designers and critics began to question the propriety of stylistic permissiveness and demanded greater accuracy, more understanding of the basic principles of each style, and even some serious consideration of the meaning and the proper use of a style. Stylistic choice became a matter of morals; association was removed from the level of romance to that of historical fact. The English architect, A. W. N. Pugin (1812–1852), equated Gothic architecture with Christian architecture. He made it his business to understand Gothic design thoroughly, and his love of Gothic led him to love the world that had produced it. In 1835 he was received into the Roman Catholic Church and about the same time he began his great work, by precept and example, of converting the Christian world to the use of the true Gothic style. He stressed the rationality of Gothic design. 'The severity of Christian architecture requires a reasonable purpose for the introduction of the smallest detail'. He insisted on a kind of honesty which had not been spoken of before and which has become one of the clichés of modern architecture: 'the external and internal appearance of an edifice should be illustrative of, and in accordance with, the purpose for which it is designed. ... Every building that is treated naturally, without disguise or concealment, cannot fail to look well.' Pugin's own buildings brought new strength and clarity to Gothic design. Apart from his writings he is best known for his collaboration with Charles Barry on the London Houses of Parliament: Barry got the commission and made the general plan, while Pugin drew all the details, from mouldings and finials to ink wells and umbrella stands. John Ruskin (1819–1900), the great critic

of art and society whose writings reached a vast public, supported Pugin's moralistic view of Gothic architecture and greatly elaborated his view of the connections between architecture and society. In *The Seven Lamps of Architecture* (1849) and *The Stones of Venice* (1851 and 1853) he made demands on the integrity of patrons and architects that were timely and effective; he also made statements that illustrate some of the flaws of even advanced Victorian artistic thought, as when he placed exclusive significance in the ornamentation of buildings, arguing that 'the only admiration worth having attached itself *wholly* to the meaning of the sculpture and colour on the building. ... What we call architecture is only the association of these in noble masses, or the placing of them in fit places. All architecture other than this is, in fact, mere *building*.' Ruskin's influence showed itself in countless Gothic buildings in the English Decorated and Italian styles he favoured. Whereas Pugin's ideas had found realisation principally in church architecture, Ruskin found himself the father of Gothic museums, railway stations and sewage plants. A more happily fruitful aspect of his writing was his insistence on 'the loving and religious labour' that produced the vitality and infinite variety of Gothic architecture.

After the climax of Neo-Classicism in the first quarter of the century, the spreading and moral transformation of the Gothic Revival dominates architectural history. These are only two aspects, however, of a complex of interrelated developments. Italian Renaissance architecture was brought into service to provide a semi-classical idiom more relaxed in feeling and more genial in its associations. National pride expressed itself in the revival of local early Renaissance styles, as also in a selective use of local variations of Gothic and Romanesque. The choice of style generally continued to vary from the comprehensible to the extravagant, as when a flax mill in Leeds, Yorkshire, was designed and built in the manner of the Egyptian temples at Philae.

The Second Half of
the Nineteenth Century

MANET AND IMPRESSIONISM

The example of Edouard Manet (1832–83) illustrates well the paradoxes that beset the realist painter. A man with a profound admiration for a considerable range of old masters and willing to base whole pictures on theirs, he is also an extreme case of a painter who looks at the world with such care that he comes to develop an idiom that appears highly artificial to people who had looked less carefully. He is represented in this book by the painting *Olympia* (1863) which he himself considered his masterpiece. It is a picture in the tradition of reclining nudes that goes back to Giorgione's *Venus*. One could account for much of it by describing it as a synthesis of elements from Giorgione, Titian, Goya, Ingres and one Jean Jalabert, who in 1842 had had great success with a picture of a nude woman attended by a negress. Yet *Olympia* was denounced with unimaginable fury when it was shown in the Salon in 1865. It was called obscene because it did not titillate the senses with hints of complaisant flesh. It was called ugly because it lacked all ingratiating modulations. It is in fact a hard painting. The frontally lit body is an almost flat shape of cream paint contrasting with the cold white of the sheet and the heavier cream of the shawl, and these are set against the dark tones of the negress, cat and background, so that one tends to see the picture as an opposition of roughly equal areas of light and dark. This works against the traditional concept of modelling and pictorial space; the public took as an affront the sharp confrontation that Manet created. That the nude, nevertheless, has remarkable solidity of form is due to the magnificent drawing and the justness of what little modelling there is: she is a painted descendant of Ingres's drawings, though an ungrateful daughter. The flatness of Manet's painting had various origins. He had studied the work of Frans Hals, of Velasquez and Goya—all of them brilliant users of blacks. He was also impressed by the flat colours and designs of the cheap Japanese prints that were beginning to attract attention in France at this time. But he was guided principally by observation, noting the two-dimensional appearance of things under certain conditions and the way the eye cannot hold in focus more than a small area of a scene. In *Olympia* the model's head is such an area, and this adds to the psychological power of the figure, again frustrating the expectations of the mid-century gallery-goer by denying access to the body.

The execrations hurled at this picture established a new 'low' in painter-public relations. 1865, we may say, marks the final consolidation of the great schism between the serious artist and his public which was a product of Romanticism and yet denies Romanticism's view of the artist as soothsayer. For Manet, who greatly desired official recognition and respectability, it was a depressing experience, but it had the effect of limelighting him as a revolutionary. The result was that a group of younger artists formed around him and looked to him as their hero.

These were the Impressionists, principally Monet, Renoir, Pissarro and Sisley. Allowing for differences in temperament, it was the aim of these painters to represent the optical character of landscape and other subjects, to the exclusion of other aspects of reality. Monet is reported to have said that he wished he had been born blind and had subsequently gained sight, so that he could have begun to paint without knowing what the objects before him were. He wanted to concern himself only with turning the rays of coloured light that struck his retina into marks of paint on the canvas. To have attitudes to the objects from which these rays come, to know about them more than the eye sees, makes this process impossible. But even if he could achieve the objectivity he wanted, there was still the problem of how to capture these fugitive optical impressions. Monet evolved what was in effect a revolutionary technique: that of covering a white canvas with juxtaposed brushstrokes of unmixed paints. The whiteness of the canvas adds to the brilliance of the colours, and these are clouded neither by mixing on the palette nor by mingling on the canvas. The Impressionists added a liking for light tones and an almost canonical aversion from black, bringing to their work a brightness that at the time seemed unbearable.

The corollaries of this kind of painting are very important, even though the painters themselves may not have been aware of them. The brushwork gave their pictures an all-over texture, as well as an all-over brightness, which led to a new kind of pictorial unity—or at least a re-establishment of the pictorial unity that had existed in medieval and early Renaissance painting until the development of chiaroscuro. The rejection of the tonal articulation of a painting was supported by their frequent use of subjects lacking a marked compositional structure. The emphasis on the brushstroke as representing light rays inhibited it from delineating forms, so that even this articulation was reduced and contemporaries found it difficult to discern the subjects of Impressionist paintings. In the name of realism the Impressionists had thus created an idiom that had to be learned before it could be read. The spectator had to trust his eyes and ignore his expectations more completely than ever before. A firm line was drawn between the perceptual character of visual art and the conceptual character of intellectual processes. But Impressionist painting also has spiritual implications, for all their eagerness to deal only in optical facts. The subjects they chose, the egalitarian way in which they painted these facts, the dominant role they awarded to light and colour as the medium revealing these facts, gave their work a quality of optimism and faith that

20

recalls the moral overtones of Constable and the Barbizon painters (from whom they learnt much), and which is particularly striking when seen against the background of self-conscious moralising implicit in many paintings by their more honoured contemporaries.

MONET, RENOIR, SISLEY AND PISSARRO

Of course there were differences between the paintings and personalities of the Impressionists—evidence, if evidence were wanted, that full objectivity is not to be achieved. Claude Monet (1840–1926) was the most ruthless of them —the first painter to reject the art of the museums in its entirety. He attempted a most extreme concentration on the objective recording of transient optical facts in his series of paintings of Rouen Cathedral and of haystacks (the undifferentiating regard he had for these subjects is typical). Between 1900 and the year of his death, Monet worked on a series of large and small paintings of his water-garden at Giverny, painting again and again the same water-lilies hovering on the water, the movements of plants below its surface and the hanging fronds of willows reflected in it. His intentions were still fundamentally the same, though his use of very large canvases (some measuring as much as $6\frac{1}{2} \times 18\frac{1}{2}$ feet), painted to hang in groups, envelop the spectator in a way that the smaller pictures by earlier nature painters could not. Moreover, as he painted the same appearances repeatedly, his brush went its own way more and more until the pictures turned into a free and wonderfully lyrical evocation of the scene rather than a conscientious description of it.

Monet had evolved the characteristic technique of Impressionist painting, and his colleagues worked in ways close to his before finding a more personal style. Auguste Renoir (1841–1919) repeatedly used the same motifs as Monet during the early years of the movement and much the same technique, but even then the feathery softness of his touch is easily distinguished from Monet's firmer placing of the paint. By inclination Renoir was really a figure painter, celebrating the beauty of women and the sweetness of friendship. He loved the old masters; it is in the museums, he said, that one learns to paint. He visited Italy several times, his first visit being in 1881. Under Italian influence he returned to a clearer delineation of forms and even adopted classical subject-matter. For a man who had passed through Impressionism this involved finding a way of uniting monumental figures with landscape, and in some of his latest paintings of broadly brushed-in nudes in heavy but generalised landscape settings, Renoir achieved this without the prettiness that weakens so much of his earlier work. Alfred Sisley (1839–99) on the whole remained closest to Impressionism proper. His are the lightest paintings, the least problematic. Camille Pissarro (1830–1903), a latecomer to painting, was the oldest of the group. His work always retained a solidity of form and construction that was not Impressionist. This, together with his warm personality, made him an ideal intermediary between the Impressionists and other painters. The most socialist among a generally left-inclined generation of artists, he liked to introduce working peasants into his landscapes, without however becoming obviously polemical.

DEGAS

The Impressionists exhibited together for the first time in 1874. By the time of the eighth and last Impressionist exhibition of 1886, most of the artists we have mentioned had ceased to participate. A considerable number of diverse painters had gathered around them. Several of them were artists of little significance; others are important but did not adopt Impressionist principles. Edgar Degas (1834–1917), for example, although habitually included in accounts of Impressionism, was a profoundly classical artist with little interest in landscape and no desire to give primacy to light. An artistic descendant of Ingres, he attached major importance to drawing and made himself one of the great draughtsmen of all time. His subject was bodily movement, or rather the interaction between the forms and tensions in a moving figure and the picture area. Here he was strongly influenced both by Japanese prints and by photography which gave him and his contemporaries a taste for random compositions. Light was one of the factors he could employ, and some of his earlier paintings have an air of indoor Impressionism about them, but on the whole he used light more to define movement than to transmit colour phenomena. There is also in his art a strong element of commentary. While there is little in it that could be called literary, we cannot escape the feeling that it is expressive of his attitude towards society. There was rarely an art more ruthlessly devoid of sentiment, more materialist in its rejection of all elements of fantasy. Degas has been accused of mysogyny. Certainly if we turn from Renoir's soft-bodied nymphets to Degas's average women caught in extreme poses, we move from pleasure-objects to images devoid of erotic promise, and from sometimes over-indulged but unexceptional sensuality to an extraordinarily relentless insistence on fact. Compared with Degas, Courbet, the self-styled Realist, is a sentimentalist. It is significant of Degas that his kindest works, those in which one feels an attachment to particular people as much as to art, are those representing prostitutes awaiting clients, celebrating Madame's birthday, and so on. Perhaps this corner of society was the one where (in the absence of clients at any rate) reality and custom met. This is not to say that Degas made it his business to work realistically in the normal sense. 'Drawing', he said, 'is not what one sees, but what others have to be made to see'; 'drawing is not form, it is the way form is seen'. For him art was a purely artificial and sophisticated means of tricking the spectator into thinking that reality lies before him. But there is also another element in Degas's art, of which he was less aware, hinted at in these successive but contradictory words: 'The artist does not draw what he sees, but what he must make others see. Only when he no longer knows what he is doing does a

17. **Edgar Degas.** *The Madame's Name-Day.* 1879. Monotype. 4¾ × 6¼ in. (12 × 16 cm.). Private collection, Paris, ex. Collection of Librairie Auguste Blaizot, Paris. Degas's graphic work joins keen observation and an extraordinary power of retention to a rare level of formal and compositional sophistication.

painter do good things'. Not only trickery, then, but also unconscious creation. Here is a partial explanation of Degas's almost obsessive use and re-use of a small range of subject-matter: as he recreated the same pictorial situation again and again, his conscious control could lessen and a deep vein of poetry open up, expressing itself through great colour harmonies that have little to do with convincing representation and nothing at all to do with Impressionist light.

POST-IMPRESSIONISM: SEURAT

Also among the non-Impressionists who contributed to Impressionist exhibitions was Georges Seurat (1859–91). As a student at the Paris Academy school, the Ecole des Beaux-Arts, Seurat had studied books on colour, optics and the affective properties of the elements of painting. In 1885 he met Pissarro, who was impressed by Seurat's scientific interests and introduced him to Impressionism. Seurat evolved a scientifically controlled version of Impressionism. Where the Impressionists had chosen paints that would resemble the colours before them, Seurat analysed each colour phenomenon into its constituent colours and set these down side by side, in dots of primary and secondary colour, to fuse in the eye by a process called optical mixture and offer a particularly vivid representation of the original colour complex. This method of painting came to be known

as Divisionism, and the group that formed round Seurat (principally Signac, Cross and Luce) came to be known as the Neo-Impressionists. But Seurat was also concerned with form. He had learned that certain kinds of form, certain directions of line, carried a particular kind of expression, and he saw it as his duty to control the formal content of his paintings as closely as the colour content. To the 1886 Impressionist exhibition he contributed what he considered his *magnum opus*, the large picture entitled *A Sunday afternoon on the Island of the Grande Jatte*. He had made a long series of studies on this island in the Seine; he had drawn and sketched in oils the figures for the picture, both out of doors and in the studio. The execution of the painting itself was a relatively mechanical process, though a very laborious one, that he could carry out day and night in his studio. It is a painting full of the monumentality that Impressionism lacked. The compositional left-right movement, stressing the picture's space, is counteracted by the figures which are grouped on clearly differentiated planes and mostly face to the left. Colours are contrasted; straight lines act against curves. There is a sufficient sense of space and bodily presence, but the picture as a whole has the simple strength of a mural.

Seurat died at the age of thirty-two. His later works show that he was developing the formal side of his work considerably and experimenting with more complex composi-

28

tions and more piquant shapes. One is tempted to speculate where this might have led. His influence was very great. His closest friend, Signac, wrote about divisionism. He and the other Neo-Impressionists did not share Seurat's great interest in formal values, and their divisionism became more and more personal and less analytical. Thus a way of painting founded in a scientific study of reality supported a tendency to a free and anti-naturalistic use of colour that became one of the foundations of modern painting. Outside Paris, Seurat's influence was first felt in Belgium where an avant-garde group calling itself *Le Groupe des XX*, formed in 1883, showed his work repeatedly and organised a Seurat retrospective exhibition in 1892. Divisionism reappears as a decisive influence in Fauvism and in Italian Futurism. In a more profound way Seurat's insistence on analysis and control is echoed in the work of Mondrian and Kandinsky.

MONUMENTAL PAINTING: PUVIS DE CHAVANNES

Seurat was not alone in looking for a monumental mode of painting to replace the informal art of Impressionism. In French literature there was a comparable shift from realism towards a more subjective and imaginative mode of writing. The dominant literary movement of the 1880s was Symbolism (Mallarmé, Rimbaud, Verlaine, etc.), which combined artificial imagery with an unprecedented exploitation of the emotive power of words and the sensory value of sounds. It was easy for those who succeeded Impressionism to overlook its poetic and moral content and to condemn it as materialism. In Cézanne's often quoted statement, 'Monet was only an eye, but, *mon Dieu*, what an eye!', the first half is as important as the second.

One of the artists much admired by Seurat and his friends, and by Cézanne, Gauguin, van Gogh and their contemporaries was Puvis de Chavannes (1824–98), a traditionalist painter who tried to combine elements of Ingres and Delacroix with the clear construction of Poussin and the directness of Italian early Renaissance murals. He never learnt the fresco technique but adapted its qualities for the oil-on-canvas murals he busily produced for public buildings in France and in the United States (Boston Public Library) between the late 1860s and his death. Apart from reminding painters of the limitations of easel painting, his murals stressed the value of flat, rhythmic design, restrained colour in light tones and a calm and constructive spirit.

27

GAUGUIN

Gauguin, for example, learned much from him. Paul Gauguin (1848–1903), the stockbroker and amateur painter who threw up his profitable career and his family for the sake of painting, and escaped first from Paris and then from Europe in search of a more spiritually vital environment, has become a legendary figure of modern art. But we are concerned with his work and his ideas about painting. His primitivism is of especial importance. Gauguin rejected, or attempted to reject, Europe's whole artistic tradition in favour of the freely expressive modes of primitive peoples. In Brittany he was influenced by the simple art of the peasants and by the flat and linear style of a much younger painter, Emile Bernard (1868–1945). A group of painters formed round him and helped to propagate his demand for an art of dream and ecstasy, and of strong and simple shapes and colours originating in the mind and not in nature: 'Work freely and madly and you will make progress. Above all, don't labour over your picture. A great emotion can be translated immediately: dream over it and look for the simplest form.' His rapture at the beauty of Tahiti ('Fabulous colours everywhere; air like fire, but pure and tranquil in its silence') led him to produce some of his finest works, rich in emotive form and colour, yet contained within a clear pictorial structure.

29

31

VAN GOGH

Vincent van Gogh (1853–90), too, has been diminished by legend: never was there a painter who was less of an inspired idiot, more of an expert. He trained himself thoroughly on the works of others; his education was wide, and the letters he wrote form the greatest literary monument left by any painter. True, he was a passionate man, but for mankind and not for himself. His efforts to serve others had been rejected and he turned to painting about 1880 as the only means left to him. His hypersensitivity to the world around him applied also to his work: to the materials of his art, the paints and brushes, the inks and reed pens, and to the pictorial elements he made his own, colour and form uniting in his linear application of dense paint. He knew colour more thoroughly and valued it more highly than any painter before him, and prophesied the great role that colour would play in the art of the future, but everything he did had its justification not in abstract knowledge but in his own thin-skinned experience. In Paris (February 1886 to February 1888) he listened to the Impressionists and adopted something of their technique, but his full flowering came in the short period he spent in the south of France. From February 1888 until his death in July 1890, in Arles, in the hospital at Saint-Rémy, and (back in the north of France) at Auvers—during twenty-nine months, interrupted by illness—he produced the great series of works that are *the* van Goghs. Light and colour were to him what they had been to Gothic artists, a form of divine revelation, and he knew that by setting certain colours against each other he could achieve an almost supernatural sonority. By heightening colour while simplifying and broadly characterising forms, he could achieve a transcendent expressiveness without losing contact with the objects he was painting. While other artists moved away from specific subject-matter towards more abstracted themes, van Gogh insisted on the uniqueness of everything he painted. His legacy is not merely a new intensity of colour, but also an intensity of expression, made all the greater by his firmly controlled manner of working and his humility before the face of nature.

30

18

18. **Vincent Van Gogh.** *Garden.* July, 1888. Pen and ink on paper. $19\frac{1}{2} \times 24$ in. (49.5 × 61 cm.). Dr Oskar Reinhart Collection, Winterthur, Switzerland. Van Gogh's elaborate and carefully controlled drawing technique provided him with a wide range of marks of differing quality with which to build up his drawings. Note the strong sense of light, yet the absence of all shading.

CÉZANNE

Cézanne is at first sight the one Post-Impressionist who remained attached to Impressionism. Pissarro's influence in the early 1870s was of great formative importance for him, but we shall see that his art aimed at and achieved qualities of which the Impressionists knew nothing. Paul Cézanne (1839–1906) studied painting in Paris but spent most of his life in and around his native town of Aix-en-Provence, painting in a seclusion and a visual environment that were very congenial to him. His early paintings are partly vehemently expressionistic visions of feasts and orgies, rich in colour and movement and owing much to Delacroix, and sometimes equally vehement but much more controlled studies of resting people and objects that owe something to Courbet and Manet. His Impressionist paintings of 1872–4, when he was working with Pissarro, have a solidity that exceeds even Pissarro's. Cézanne never adopted the Impressionists' interest in light and colour as the visible form of nature. He adapted their technique, placing brushstrokes side by side on his canvases, and their example led him to paint landscape. But whereas they were concerned with the constantly changing face of nature and

their way of painting was evolved to cope with this instability, Cézanne dealt with a much more complex theme: the stability of things as well as their instability, their conceptual as well as optical value, their reality as well as the reality of the paint on his canvas.

There are many recorded statements by Cézanne, and it is characteristic of him that some of them seem to contradict others. The most revealing explanation he gave of his work was the one recorded by Bernard: 'I have my motif. (He joins his hands.) A motif, you see, is this. (He draws his hands apart, fingers spread out, and brings them together again, slowly; then joins them, presses them together and contracts them, making them interlace.) There you have it; that is what one must attain.' In other words: the integration on the canvas of many-sided reality, nothing escaping. The process was slow and intuitive, involving much observation and then the deliberate establishment of certain cardinal points on the canvas as footholds in a region to be conquered. 'To paint is not merely to copy the object; it is

33

(Continued on page 65)

22, 23. **Claude Monet.** *Springtime.* 1874
(above). Oil on canvas. $22\frac{1}{2} \times 31\frac{1}{2}$ in.
(57×80.5 cm.). Staatsgemäldesamm-
lungen, Berlin-Dahlem. **Alfred Sisley.**
Barge during the Flood. 1876 (right). Oil
on canvas. $19\frac{3}{4} \times 24$ in. (50×61 cm.).
Musée de l'Impressionnisme, Paris.
Impressionism can be seen as a kind of
water-shed between traditional and
modern painting. The Impressionists'
intention was to capture the visual
qualities of a scene. They developed a
pictorial shorthand that increased the
speed of painting, gave much greater
luminosity to their pictures, and was
sufficiently open not to contradict the
transience of nature's appearance. Thus
they attempted a more absolute realism
than that of the past and showed that
academic techniques could only deal with
a very limited naturalism. But Impressionism too is a limited and an artificial
language, since it involves exclusive attention to the optical values of a scene at the
expense of the observer's conceptual
knowledge of the world and his emotional
relationship to it.

24. **Claude Monet.** *Water-lilies
(Nymphéas).* 1904. Oil on canvas.
35½ × 36¼ in. (90 × 92 cm.). Musée de
l'Impressionnisme, Paris. During the last
twenty years of his life, Monet repeatedly
painted the water garden he had himself
created at Giverny, near Paris. In his
pictures of this subject, often very large,
his Impressionist technique softens and
broadens, and, as he approaches the pool
with its water-lilies more and more closely,
the pictures lose all controlling structure
apart from that offered by the forms and
colours of his brushstrokes, until they
become scarcely legible as representations
of a place and take on an independent
existence as painted surfaces that are rich
in colour offering strangely ambiguous
sensations of space.

25. **Pierre Auguste Renoir.** *Nude in the
Sunlight. c.* 1875–6. Oil on canvas.
31½ × 25½ in. (80 × 61 cm.). Musée de
l'Impressionnisme, Paris. More than the
other Impressionists, Renoir concerned
himself with the human figure and thus
joined Impressionism to the long tradition
of art celebrating physical beauty.

27. **Pierre Puvis de Chavannes.** *The Sacred Grove.* 1883–4. Oil mural. 180 × 418 in. (458 × 1062 cm.). Musée des Beaux-Arts, Lyon. Painted in pale colours to suggest the appearance of fresco painting, the paleness of Puvis' murals also contributes to their calmness, clarity and two-dimensional coherence. After the Baroque tendencies of Romantic painting, the work of Puvis drew attention to the values of clear design and pictorial reticence.

26. **Edgar Degas.** *After the Bath (La Sortie de Bain). c.* 1895–8. Pastel. 30 × 32½ in. (76 × 82.5 cm.). Phillips Collection, Washington. Degas is often grouped with the Impressionists, but his aims were much more complex. Although concerned in general with optical impressions in terms both of light and colour, he was particularly interested in the quality of movement in the human body and the structural relationship between the movement and tensions of the figure in relation to the picture as a whole.

28. **Georges Seurat.** *Sunday Afternoon on the Island of the Grande Jatte.* 1885–6. Oil on canvas. 81 × 120¾ in. (205.5 × 305.5 cm.). Courtesy of the Art Institute of Chicago, Helen Birch Bartlett Memorial Collection. One of the greatest monuments of nineteenth-century painting, this picture marks the meeting point between the naturalism of much of the art of that century, and the structural and psychological concerns of much twentieth-century art. Seurat was twenty-six when he began this painting which represents the fullest realisation of his ideas at that time. At the time of his death, his work seemed to be taking a new direction.

29. **Emile Bernard.** *Breton Women in the Meadow (Bretonnes dans la Prairie)*. 1888. Oil on canvas. $29\frac{1}{8} \times 36\frac{1}{4}$ in. (74×92 cm.). Collection: Maurice-Denis, Saint-Germain-en-Laye. Bernard's fame has been obscured by that of Gauguin. Bernard had painted this picture before Gauguin met him in Brittany, and it led Gauguin to strengthen his colours, simplify his colour areas and use firmly painted outlines—that is, to suppress the Impressionist elements in his work. Subsequently Bernard's stylised art became one of the sources of Art Nouveau; compare this illustration with van de Velde's embroidery, plate 32.

30. **Vincent van Gogh.** *Self-portrait with Bandaged Ear.* 1889. Oil on canvas. $23\frac{1}{2} \times 19\frac{1}{4}$ in. (60×49 cm.). Courtauld Institute Gallery, London. Painted in January, 1889, about three weeks after his attack on Gauguin and subsequent self-mutilation, this work demonstrates both the control and the power of van Gogh's art. The form and direction of the brush-strokes recreate the structure of the subject painted, and at the same time weld the picture into a tightly constructed whole.

31. **Paul Gauguin.** *Where Do We Come From? What Are We? Where Are We Going?* 1897. 54¾ × 147½ in. (139 × 374.5 cm.). Courtesy Museum of Fine Arts, Boston. 'I believe not only that this canvas surpasses in value all my previous ones, but that I shall never make a better or a similar one. I have put into it before dying all my energy, a passion so painful in terrible circumstances, and a vision so clear, needing no corrections, that the hastiness disappears and life surges up.'

32. **Henri van de Velde.** *Engelswachen.* 1891. Tapestry. 55 × 91¾ in. (139.5 × 233 cm.). Kunstgewerbe Museum, Zürich. One of the first Art Nouveau painters to abandon fine art, Van de Velde became a leading architect, designer and theorist.

33. **Paul Cézanne.** *The Turning Road.* *(La Route Tournante).* 1879–82. Oil on canvas. 23½ × 28¾ in. (60 × 73 cm.). Courtesy Museum of Fine Arts, Boston. Impressionism led Cézanne to paint landscapes in the open air, but he strove to integrate forms and light and construct his pictures with the solidity of the old masters.

34. **Paul Cézanne.** *Bathers (La Grande
Baignade)*. 1898–1905. Oil on canvas.
82 × 98¼ in. (208 × 249.5 cm.). Museum
of Art, Philadelphia. (Wistach Collection).
The largest of Cézanne's series of bathers,
this picture represents his most ambitious
attempt to submit the human figure to
the kind of reconstruction he imposed on
landscape and still-life subjects, and to
distort it to fit his structural and expressive
purpose without diminishing its presence
or dignity.

35. **Odilon Redon.** *Cyclops*. *c.* 1898. Oil
on panel. 25¼ × 20 in. (64 × 50.8 cm.).
Rijksmuseum Kröller-Müller, Otterlo.
The development of Symbolist poetry
coincided with a tendency towards fantastic art which found its finest expression
in the lithographs and pictures of Redon,
who thus stands out as a forerunner of
Surrealism.

36. **Henri Marie Raymond de Toulouse-Lautrec.** *Divan Japonais.* 1892. Poster. Lithograph. 31 × 23½ in. (60 × 80 cm.). Musée Toulouse-Lautrec, Albi. Through his lithographs, for use as posters etc., Toulouse-Lautrec brought painting and commercial art into a particularly close relationship which continued through the Art Nouveau period. Since then the interchange has been more spasmodic.

37. **Pierre Bonnard.** *Le Café. c.* 1914. Oil on canvas. 28¾ × 41⅞ in. (73 × 106.5 cm.). Reproduced by courtesy of the Trustees of the Tate Gallery, London. In his contributions to the long history of paintings of domestic scenes, Bonnard achieves a transformation of the physical world into an independent pictorial world of colour and tone that is comparable to that of Monet in his late works.

38. **James Ensor.** *Intrigue.* 1890. Oil on canvas. 35½ × 59 in. (90 × 150 cm.). Musée Royal des Beaux-Arts, Antwerp. Having had some succes with beautifully painted domestic and outdoor scenes, Ensor rejected agreeable subject-matter and pleasant techniques and colours to use his art as a weapon to criticise the world about him, particularly its hypocrisy.

39. **Edvard Munch.** *Jealousy.* 1896 or 1897. Oil on canvas. 26½ × 39⅜ in. (67 × 100 cm.). Billedgalleri, Bergen. Reproduced by courtesy of the Munch Museet, Oslo. This work relates to specific events in Munch's own life, and is typical of his adaptation of a more or less Art Nouveau idiom for intensely subjective and expressive purposes.

40. **Hans von Marées.** *The Hesperides II.*
1884–5. Tempera on panel. 134 × 190 in.
(340 × 482 cm.). Bayerische Staatsgemäldesammlungen, Munich. While the
Post-Impressionists were challenging
naturalism in the name of organisation and
expression, the German painter Marées
sought monumentality and cohesion
through simplified classicism, a firm
structure, and a harmonious interrelation
of idealised forms and a few colours.

41. **Max Liebermann.** *The Cobbler's
Workshop.* 1881. Oil on canvas. 25 × 31½
in. (64 × 80 cm.). Nationalgalerie, East
Berlin. Impressionism was denounced in
Prussia as an art of rebellion and its influence led to a schism in the Berlin
Artists' Society in 1892. Liebermann was
recognised as the leader of German Impressionism but he adopted only some
aspects of it, and joined them to the kind
of realism he had seen in Dutch seventeenth-century painting.

42. **James McNeill Whistler.** *Arrangement in Grey, (self-portrait).* 1871–3. Oil on canvas. 29½ × 21 in. (75 × 53.5 cm.). Institute of Arts, Detroit. In Paris Whistler was affected by Manet and Japanese art. From 1859 in London, his work displays a self-justifying aesthetic delicacy that borders at times on vapidity but has an extraordinarily fine sense of composition and tonal values.

43. **William Morris.** *Daisy wallpaper.* 1862. Wood-block on paper. 27 × 21 in. (68.5 × 53.5 cm.). Victoria and Albert Museum, London. Morris's emphasis on flat design in applied arts is closely contemporary with Manet's rejection of three-dimensional effects in painting.

44. **Gustav Klimt.** *The Kiss.* 1908 or 1911. Oil on canvas. 71 × 71 in. (180 × 180 cm.). Österreichische Galerie, Vienna. The greatest of Art Nouveau painters, Klimt (1862–1918) made bold use of large contrasting areas of colours and pattern to produce almost barbaric splendour.

to seize a harmony between numerous relationships'. He sought the tensions between objects as well as their physical presence as part of the pictorial tension of forms on the canvas. Portraits he found troublesome, not only because sitters could hardly manage the immobility he demanded, but also because of the complex psychological relationships that he had to command as well as everything else; hence the famous occasion when he impatiently told his posing wife, 'Be an apple!'

As time went on Cézanne's art became ever more gentle and tentative. His figure subjects culminated in the *Grande*
34 *Baignade* of his last years, but generally speaking his work became less monumental and more totally integrated. Like Turner, he adapted watercolour methods for his oil painting, leaving gaps between the thin washes of increasingly economical colour. Yet, fragmentary and insubstantial as his later paintings often look, they embody the subject's reality, the painter's experience of the subject and his regard for the picture as a two-dimensional object bearing upon it touches of colour.

Cézanne's importance lies in his position as the meeting point of disparate traditions. Cubism and Fauvism owe much to him and countless painters have regarded him as their 'master *par excellence*' (as Klee wrote). Behind him lies the painterly tradition of Veronese, Rubens, Watteau, Delacroix, and the French classical tradition of Poussin, Chardin and Ingres. He is linked to Seurat in his concern for a clear structure on the picture plane, and to van Gogh by his regard for the value of the objects and the need to 'realise' them. He spoke of 'realising his little sensation' and meant by this, constructing a convincing pictorial image containing the live character of his motif and yet preserving the reality of the painting itself as an object made of paints and canvas. Like an Impressionist he underlines the unity of things, but in terms of interrelationships, not under a blanket of light. And when he flattened pictorial space, stressing the surface of his picture with his mosaic-like touches of paint, adjusting the forms of three-dimensional objects to bring them to the surface, and rejecting (with the help of the Provençal climate) the possibility of atmospheric veils distancing the horizon, he was not applying a pre-conception or a dogma: he was observing, with a patience and an objectivity that are quite unequalled. Perhaps we can see, in this patience and this objectivity, his earlier turbulence harnessed to a clearer creative purpose. No longer is his passion seen in explosive subjects or their dramatic presentation; now, so to speak, it comes between the brushstrokes, in the act of looking, in the long process

of weighing up and selecting. Cézanne did not beget a movement, yet he knew he was the progenitor of a new art and almost all painting since his day has owed something to him. His recognition that 'art is a harmony parallel to nature' is the foundation of all subsequent developments.

OTHER POST-IMPRESSIONISTS

Cézanne, Gauguin, Seurat and van Gogh are usually grouped together as the Post-Impressionists, but they share not so much a style as a negative attitude towards Impressionism. Associated with these giants, there were also relatively minor figures who made important contributions. The Nabi group based itself principally on the ideas of Gauguin and Bernard, and developed particularly their use of flat coloured shapes into decorative idioms that influenced the Art Nouveau movement. One of them, Maurice Denis, published in 1890 the challenging statement that became a rallying cry: 'Remember that a picture, before being a battle horse, a nude woman or some anecdote, is essentially a flat surface covered with colours assembled in a certain order'. Two of them, Edouard Vuillard (1868–1940) and Pierre Bonnard (1867–1947) started from such a decorative style and added to it elements from Impressionism in paintings of domestic scenes. 'The pain-   37
ter's instrument is his armchair', said Vuillard, and they found in their homes complexes of light and dark, of linear structure and colour patterns of extraordinary visual interest. After 1900 Bonnard came to use more intense colours for pictures full of optical incident. To his interiors he added a series of resplendent landscapes, firmly constructed but wonderfully rich and fluid. Odilon Redon (1840–1916)   35
was the painter most directly associated with Symbolism. 'Everything takes form,' he said, 'when we meekly submit to the uprush of the unconscious', thus stating with precision a view that has become the programme of many later painters. His close study of nature, of colour, and of the techniques of painting and lithography, enabled him to present his fantasies with great technical and imaginative freedom.

BELGIAN AND GERMAN PAINTING

Outside France, too, there were painters struggling away from the emphasis on natural appearances that dominated so much nineteenth-century painting. The Belgian, James Ensor (1860–1949), one of the *Groupe des XX*, turned away   38
from the sensitive recording of the world around him and directed his work to criticise that world. He rejected not only naturalism but also traditional standards of fine painting, adopting a cartoonish manner that led even his friends of *Les XX* to exclude him from their exhibitions. The Norwegian, Edvard Munch (1863–1944), who studied partly in Paris and then spent some years in Berlin, used his art to express (and thus in part surmount) his profound personal disturbances that made his streets echo with fear, filled landscape with death and turned woman into a vampire.   39
Both Ensor and Munch were to exercise much influence on

45. **Antonio Gaudi.** *Church of the Holy Family, Barcelona.*
Gothic in its general silhouette, Art Nouveau in its tendency to curves and elaborate ornamentation rather than straight lines, and profoundly original in its structural basis, Gaudi's church, even in its sadly incomplete state, is a monumental milestone on architecture's road from historicism to a new expressiveness and functionalism.

the central European movements labelled Expressionism, both as painters and as graphic artists.

In Germany academic naturalism had joined with literary sentimentalism to rot the moral fibres of painting. Among the handful of painters fighting to lift their art to a higher level through style and seriousness, the most impressive was Hans von Marées (1837–87). He spent most of his life in Italy, adopting the classical ideal of a Golden Age in order to concern himself first and foremost with pictorial organisation. He was the only German painter of the century to comprehend the constructive power of colour, and with his broad colour chords and clear linear structures, composed large paintings that have a real sense of the monumental. His country lacked an artistic past on which to establish new standards (until the Expressionists managed to strike roots into the age of Dürer) and it took little interest in Marées's abstraction. To this day he is little regarded outside Germany, perhaps the most underrated painter of his century.

IMPRESSIONISM OUTSIDE FRANCE

The general effect of Impressionism in Europe was an involvement with realistic tendencies, lending them a greater freshness of colour and technique. In Germany painters like Max Liebermann (1847–1935), Corinth and Slevogt, worked on the basis of a brusque naturalism in which elements of Barbizon painting, Manet, Courbet and Impressionism mingled. James Abbott McNeill Whistler (1834–1903), American born, Paris trained, but working principally in London, came close to Impressionism in some of his less abstract works. But Manet, Spanish painting and Japanese prints were at least equally important to him, and his ideal was an entirely artifial art that owed little to observation of nature. He said, 'As music is the poetry of sound, so painting is the poetry of sight, and the subject-matter has nothing to do with the harmony of sound or of colour', and he stressed the importance of our, so to speak, listening to his paintings by giving them titles that refer to music, *Nocturne*, *Symphony*, *Harmony*. He was a fine colourist, but it was in the tonal construction of his paintings that he was at his best, and he should be remembered as the last great disposer of tone. Real Impressionism was less well received in Britain than might have been expected. English taste in landscape painting still inclined to the picturesque. The public, at last accustomed to Constable and the earlier works of Turner, on the whole found Impressionism too aggressive in colour and too wild in technique. The word, 'Impressionist', was attached to some English painters but their version of the style, as in the case of Philip Wilson Steer, was dominated by the English landscape tradition or, as in the case of Walter Richard Sickert (1860–1942), owed more to marginal figures like Degas than to the movement itself. Nevertheless the broken touch of Impressionism, its fresh colouring and adherence to everyday subject-matter entered deeply into European art consciousness; the very way in which we look at our en-

vironment has been altered by what was once generally agreed to be the work of incompetent anarchists.

ART NOUVEAU

Yet even as the ripples of French influence spread this new naturalism, a broad movement swept across Europe, owing much to Post-Impressionism but ranging widely over the fine and applied arts and architecture. Known as Art Nouveau in France and Britain and as *Jugendstil* in Germany, it represented the first new international style since the Middle Ages owing nothing to historicism. It is not principally a style of painting, although it derived some of its characteristics from aspects of Post-Impressionism and helped to spread these into the painting of other countries, but in its varying manifestations it placed great emphasis on the power of lines and colours irrespective of subject-matter and even showed such elements could control the character of a whole environment. Stylistically a limited and short-lived movement, it was one of the forces that pushed later painting towards abstraction. Its immediate effect was to link the several centres where Art Nouveau flourished—notably Paris, Munich, Brussels, Vienna, Glasgow and Moscow—and to encourage pure artists to apply their sensibilities to design. During the height of Art Nouveau, roughly 1895–1905, a great number of painters turned from studio to workshop activities, like, for example, the Belgian, Henry van de Velde (1863–1957), who began as a Neo-Impressionist painter, then designed furniture and interiors, then worked as architect, and is perhaps most important for his work as teacher in Germany (Weimar) and Belgium (Brussels and Ghent). Generally speaking, Art Nouveau had the effect of encouraging artists to trust

19 (left). **Jan Toorop.** *Girl with Swans (Dolce). c.* 1896. Coloured lithograph. 9¼ × 7¾ in. (23.5 × 19.5 cm.). Rijksprenten-Kabinet, Amsterdam. The patterns of flowers and parallel lines, and the exaggerated quality of sub-Pre-Raphaelite languidness, make this print an extreme but by no means unique example of international Art Nouveau design.

20, 21. **Auguste Rodin.** *St John the Baptist preaching.* 1878. Bronze. 79 × 21¾ × 38¾ in. (200 × 55 × 98 cm.). Musée Rodin, Paris. *Polyphemus.* 1888. Bronze. 9¾ × 5½ × 6¼ in. (25 × 14 × 16 cm.). Musée Rodin, Paris. Rodin sought powerful expression rather than beauty. To achieve this he moved far from naturalism and even further from ideal standards of beauty. Often he gave his figures poses involving extreme physical tension in order to express spiritual states, and he broke up his sculptures' surfaces to enliven and dramatise the form.

in their own inventiveness and to ally themselves less to recognised styles. Art Nouveau and Post-Impressionism form the platform on which twentieth-century painters were to build.

LATER NINETEENTH-CENTURY SCULPTURE: RODIN AND OTHERS

The history of sculpture in the second half of the century is brighter than that of the first: in Rodin, France produced a sculptor of outstanding quality and importance. But he stands alone. Around him the art of sculpture reaches unprecedented depths, while hero-worship and rampant nationalism combine to guarantee demand. The few sculptors we need recall are almost exclusively French.

Jean-Baptiste Carpeaux (1827–75) can be seen as a follower of Rude, extending the latter's Baroque Romanticism into a lighter and at times more realistic vein that could be called Rococo Romanticism. A comparison of Carpeaux's relief *The Dance* (1869) on the Paris Opéra with Rude's relief on the Arc de Triomphe shows the greater delicacy of Carpeaux's work, though it is doubtful whether this recommends it as sculpture for an architectural setting.

Sculpture played a similar role for Degas as it had for Daumier. He made a considerable series of wax studies of dancers, bathers and horses, as alternatives to sketches done on paper, his aim being to seize the character of a pose and its involvement with the surrounding space.

20, 21, **17**   Rodin alone achieved a really significant relationship with the past and the future. Auguste Rodin (1840–1917) was not naturally a revolutionary. He sought and gained public approbation and there were streaks in him of the sentimentalism that falsifies so much nineteenth-century art. He was more vehemently for the past than other sculptors and did not limit his enthusiasm to the classical tradition, taking a passionate interest in Gothic art and seeing Michelangelo as 'the culmination of all Gothic thought'. All his work was concerned with the human figure. He had the original idea (inspired by classical remains) of making truncated figures, limbless and/or headless torsos which were thought in his day to reveal a streak of sadism (as perhaps they do), but have the important effect of lifting sculpture out of the range of normal subject-matter into a sphere where its abstract qualities of line, mass and tension dominate the responses it evokes. Rodin, who admired and encouraged Degas as a sculptor, went far beyond him in his search for the unposed pose. Degas was fascinated by the ritual gestures of women at their toilet, by the conventional movements of ballet dancers on stage and their almost as conventional movements off it, and he accepted gladly any deviations from his selected norms. Rodin planned for deviations. His models moved around him and he captured in swift line-and-wash sketches those momentary dispositions that seemed to him expressive. Thus, like Michelangelo, he found in artistically unprecedented movements a whole world of expressive form that seemed to him fundamentally at one with nature at large: 'A woman, a mountain or a horse are formed according to the same principles'. He was an expressionist before Expressionism. His means were often those of exaggeration, and he received into art figures and themes that were generally considered ugly and therefore unsuitable: 'in art only those things that are characterless are ugly'.

The range of Rodin's work is in itself impressive: from marbles laboriously worked by assistants to swift terracotta sketches, from incomplete torsos to the encyclopedic project (left unfinished but productive of several separate sculptures) of the *Gate of Hell*. The open surfaces of his bronzes suggest vivid sensations of life and mobility. In particular the surfaces of his smallest and improvised works, exhibited mostly after 1900, liberated sculptors from the strait-jacket of 'finish'. There was much opposition to his work in his day, but his influence was such that he alone can be thought of as the father of modern sculpture.

His exclusive attachment to the human body, however, limited his effectiveness in history. A great part of modern sculpture is concerned with other kinds of form and with questions of form unrelated to anthropometry. Here Rodin did offer one important precept: 'sculpture is the art of the hole and the lump', which could be taken as the underlying theme of much subsequent work, but he had little to say about sculpture as structure. Here lies the importance of Marées's friend, the sculptor, Adolf von Hildebrand (1847–1921), who insisted that sculpture is a visual art that must

22. **Edgar Degas.** *Dancer Looking at the Sole of her Right Foot.* 1910–11. Bronze. 18¾ in. high (47.5 cm.). Reproduced by courtesy of the Trustees of the Tate Gallery, London. Clay was to Degas an ideal means for studying and capturing the character of a momentary pose.

be organised to present itself clearly to sight. The sculptor's problem, he said, was that of 'unifying forms into relief effects'. 'So long as the chief effect of any plastic figure is its reality as a solid, it is imperfect as a work of art'. His own work is marked by impassivity and clarity, and by a simplification of forms that has been rendered commonplace by the host of his followers. Did Hildebrand sense the dichotomy of reality and unreality we mentioned earlier, and seek to reduce it? Historically his most important work is the treatise, *The Problem of Form* (1893), one of the few books ever written to question the functions of sculpture. Its influence reached not only sculptors but artists and writers on art generally.

The Italian sculptor, Medardo Rosso (1858–1928), in a   *24* different way also stressed the non-physical character of

23. **Adolf von Hildebrand.** *Male Nude.* 1884. Marble. 69 in. high (175 cm.). Staatliche Museen, East Berlin. Without denying the values of the classical tradition, Hildebrand struggled to bring clarity and firmness into an art sadly depreciated by the countless exercises in imitation classicism produced in his century.

24. **Medardo Rosso.** *The Bookmaker,* or *Portrait of Monsieur M.M.* 1894 (original). Wax over plaster. 17½ in. (44.5 cm.). Collection of G. Mattioli, Milan. Rosso's glimpse of a moving figure approximates to the objective records of Impressionist painting and at the same time proposes a new formal language, imprecise but expressive.

sculpture. Under the influence of the Impressionists, he modelled small sculptures affecting all the transience and indistinctness of form and the chance positions that they used in their pictures. To a long term view this seems an evasion of rather than a solution to the problems of sculpture, but historically Rosso played the interesting role of forming a bridge between Impressionism and the Futurists of his own country, and demonstrated in sculpture what has since become a stock theme of modern art aesthetics: 'We should accustom ourselves to seeing in movement the clearest and the simplest thing there is, since rest is merely the most extreme limit of the deceleration of movement, perhaps only an ideal limit that is never realised in nature.' (Bergson, 1901).

LATER NINETEENTH-CENTURY ARCHITECTURE

The bad architecture of the latter half of the nineteenth century is more dismal than that of the former, when there were still traditions of taste to guide designer and patron, but the good architecture is more adventurous than anything since Soane and Schinkel. Historicism was far from dead but there was a growing desire among architects to stop treating architecture as an art of imitation. The two outstanding developments of this period are the impact of cast iron and steel and the search for a kind of architectural primitivism not unlike that we have noticed in painting. In both respects America takes on a very important role.

It was a failure on the part of professional architects to meet a specific architectural problem that led to the creation of one of the most revolutionary buildings of the century. When the building committee for London's Great Exhibition of 1851 had finished its designs, it was clear that insufficient time remained for its erection. The solution came from the Duke of Devonshire's head gardener,

25 (above). **Sir Joseph Paxton.** *Crystal Palace, London.* 1850–51
A totally successful invasion of the field of architecture by the
forces of engineering and manufacture, this exhibition building
was honoured by later generations as a unique forerunner of
the technological architecture that is now coming into being.

26. **Lewis Cubitt.** *King's Cross Station, London.* 1851–52. Cubitt's
station shows considerable structural boldness but is outstanding
for the undisguised demonstration of its basic structure on the
front of the building, where another architect would have
preferred to veil the engineering structure of the platform
sheds with a façade of white-collared classical or Gothic
architecture.

27. **Henri Labrouste.** *Reading Room, Bibliothèque Nationale, Paris.* 1862–8. Whilst Labrouste still found it necessary to pay homage to tradition in his ornament, the fine lines of his metal and terracotta vaults on their slender columns give his Reading Room a new lightness and space.

25 Joseph Paxton (1803–65), who designed what became known as the Crystal Palace on the basis of ideas he had already applied to the design of glass and cast-iron greenhouses. Erected in nine months out of mass-produced and standard ingredients that could be taken down as easily as set up, the vast Crystal Palace offered new experiences in architectural light and space as a convincing demonstration of the utility of new materials and industrial techniques. The exhibition inside it demonstrated at once the wonders of international manufacture and the depths to which design had sunk at the time. To permit the enclosing of a great elm, Paxton had inserted a vaulted transept into his original design, its glass vaults supported on laminated wood arches.

26 This system was also used to carry the two glass vaults over a cast-iron substructure at King's Cross Station, London (designed by Lewis Cubitt in 1850; and built 1851–2). The station has a special place in history because of the way

in which these vaults (that is, the utilitarian engineering structure) are boldly displayed at the main front of the station where it was normal to have recourse to historical rhetoric. In Paris, where the discreet use of cast iron to strengthen masonry has a long history, the Reading Room of the Bibliothèque Nationale (by Henri Labrouste, 1801– 27 75; built 1862–8) is an outstanding example of an interior dominated by a very thinly disguised cast-iron structure of great elegance. The process invented by Bessemer in 1855, facilitating the large-scale production of steel, offered new possibilities for the use of metal in building. Gustave Eiffel's 28 (1832–1923) tower, built for the Paris Exhibition of 1889 and nearly a thousand feet high, celebrates the fact. Until the erection of the Empire State Building in New York in the early 1930s, the Eiffel Tower remained the tallest structure in the world. For the same exhibition the engineer, Contamin (1840–93), erected the Palais des Machines, a 30 masterpiece of engineering.

28. **Gustave Eiffel.** *Viaduct over the Truyère at Garabit.* 1880–4.
The creator of the Eiffel Tower in 1887–9 had previously had
two major opportunities to test the potential of the lattice-beam
he had developed: in a bridge over the Douro near Oporto,
Portugal, and in this soaring structure in the French Massif
Central.

29, 31 (left and right). **Louis Sullivan.** *Guaranty Building, Buffalo, New York,* and *exterior detail* (left). 1894–5. Sullivan's office buildings show his feeling both for structure as a source of architectural expression and for localised ornamentation of a delicate and complex kind.

30 (left). Engineers: **Contamin, Pierre & Charton.** Associated Architect, **Dutert.** *Palais des Machines, Paris International Exhibition.* 1889. Steel and glass. Span 375 ft., length 1,400 ft. (114.3 m. × 426.7 m.). A heroic demonstration of the functional potential of steel and glass engineering, this exhibition hall helped also to develop a new sense of formal beauty.

It is the American steel-framed skyscraper, however, that marks the true conjunction of architecture and engineering and the moment when architects begin to accept engineering structures as part of the forces they command. From about 1890 onwards, skyscrapers arose in Chicago and New York in quick succession. Louis Sullivan (1856–1924) was the most thoughtful and inventive architect to contribute to this development. The dictum he propagated, that 'form follows function', is neither unprecedented nor a sufficient explanation of his work, which was as much concerned with new ideas in abstract ornamentation (linking Sullivan to the Art Nouveau movement) and with self-justifying formal effects as with the logic of structure and function. One of his finest office blocks is the Guaranty Building in Buffalo, New York (1894–5). Here the cage-like structure is dramatically expressed on the exterior,

even hinting in the openness of the ground floor at the later convention of raising buildings on piers or *pilotis*. The upper storeys rejoice in the verticality of the structure instead of countermanding it. The cornice-like projection at the top and the ornamental terracotta cladding represent the other side of Sullivan's interests.

THE REJECTION OF HISTORICISM

The freedom from historical styles shown by Sullivan's work—the freedom, that is, for architects to form each building according to its needs and his time's inclinations—was successfully reasserted during the later decades of the century. It was not the work of one architect and manifested itself in different ways, but it always involved the rejection of the heavy historical styles that flourished in the middle of the century and an almost total aversion from the

32 (left). **William Butterfield.** *All Saints' Church, Margaret Street, London.* 1849–59. Butterfield is an outstanding example of those few mid-century architects who were able to bring to Gothic design an inventiveness comparable to that with which Soane and a few others handled the classical idiom earlier.

34 (right). **Philip Webb.** *The Red House, Bexley Heath, Kent.* 1859–60. This house, which was built for William Morris, is an early example of the almost styleless primitivism that could result from a personal and more or less functional use of traditional idioms.

33 (below). **Richard Norman Shaw.** *Leyswood, Groombridge, Sussex.* 1868–9. Pen drawing. 22½ × 33½ in. (57 × 85 cm.). The Drawing Collection, Royal Institute of British Architects, London. To Shaw and to other architects of his generation, a personal and functional use of pre-Renaissance design traditions appeared to offer a way out of the historicism that had vitiated so much nineteenth-century architecture.

associative evaluation of past styles for the sake of more purely aesthetic responses. Historicism itself contributed by drawing attention to periods of architecture when effects of massing, of texture or bareness, of void set against solid, etc., dominated over conventional ornament. The simpler forms of medieval architecture, and particularly of Romanesque buildings, were important here, and contributions came also from the traditions of peasant building, farms, cottages and barns, and generally from local traditions that had arisen without benefit of white-collared professionalism. Thus architecture was affected by the same search for the primitive basis of design that we observed in the works of the Pre-Raphaelites and that of Gauguin and his friends, and this search becomes even more characteristic of developments after 1900.

32   Here again Britain played a leading role. Butterfield's very personal use of Gothic forms in the 1840s and 1850s appears to have emboldened others. From about 1860, a number of British architects designed buildings in which historical elements play only a minor part. Richard Nor-
33 man Shaw (1831–1912) used various late-medieval and Renaissance styles but handled them in an original and picturesque way. His buildings are curiously timeless and have a relaxed quality that contrasts absolutely with the gesturing of so much Victorian design. His career suggests that there was a considerable demand for his informal buildings. Philip Webb (1831–1915), a more sensitive but less famous architect, produced a masterpiece of organic
34 architecture in his Red House. It looks as though it had been evolved rather than designed. Some of its forms hint at Gothic architecture, and steep tiled roofs and fine brick-

work indicate the North, while its timeless quality is even more marked than in Shaw's work. Also Webb's feeling for materials and craftsmanship is greatly superior to Shaw's.

MORRIS

Red House was built for William Morris (1834–96), perhaps the greatest regenerative force in art and design of his time. Morris had studied architecture and had then turned to painting under the influence of Rossetti. In disgust at the aesthetic and technical quality of the furnishings available to him when Red House was being built, he decided to use things produced by his friends and by himself. Out of this grew the firm of Morris, Marshall, Faulkner and Company, through which he hoped to reform design and influence the whole world of labour. He was inspired by Pugin and Ruskin, and by his passionate and practical regard for the Middle Ages as an age when over-specialisation had not yet deprived man of joy in his work. His own artistic talent lay in two-dimensional design, particularly in the repeating designs needed for wallpapers and fabrics. 43
These are often outstanding, though not quite as revolutionary as has sometimes been thought. His designs were in fact widely appreciated, partly because he was already well-known as a Romantic poet, but it was not Morris's purpose to provide Victorian gentlefolk with pretty walls. He was a critic of society. He took up Ruskin's theme, that capitalism had turned work into labour, and developed it in writings that began in 1877 and were soon read in Europe and America. Wholesome work had been turned into mindless drudgery, he argued, when the process of making one thing had been split into separate actions. In matters

35. Frank Lloyd Wright. *Ward Willits House, Illinois.* 1902.
In his 'Prairie Houses', of which this is one, Wright grouped the
rooms around a chimney-stack core, allowing space to flow
from one to the next and extending the house outwards by
means of porches. The functional simplicity of these houses
attracted a great deal of attention in Europe after 1910.

of applied art, not only did no one person have the satisfaction of making a complete thing, but the act of conceiv-
ing and designing it was left to yet another person who
could be totally unaware of the special problems involved
in carrying out his design. The development of the machine
had sectionalised and impersonalised the manufacturing
process even further. The enemy was blind commercialism,
and socialism the antidote.

Although Morris studied the processes involved in producing the things he designed, he could not reintegrate
design and manufacture. What he did manage to establish,
and his Arts and Crafts Movement propagate, was a new
regard for crafts and for craftsmen and the need to relate
design to function and material. He partly bridged, that is,
the division between the fine artist and the craftsman that
the Renaissance had struggled to achieve, and he partly
freed the decorative arts from their subservience to the
canons of fine art. In 1880 he wrote: 'Have nothing in your
houses that you do not know to be useful, or believe to be
beautiful', and he and his friends worked towards making
adherence to this principle possible. Later, in 1891, Morris
started the Kelmscott Press to bring the same standard into
printing and illustration. His failure was that of the society
in which he lived: all his work only served to make the rich
more comfortable. 'I do not want art for a few, any more
than education for a few, or freedom for a few. No, rather
than art should live this poor thin life among a few excep-

tional men, ... I would that the world should indeed sweep
away all art for awhile.'

THE UNITED STATES

The revitalisation of picturesque design seen in the work of
Webb, Shaw and their successors, was echoed in America,
particularly in the activity of Henry Hobson Richardson
(1838–86). Richardson's strong and masculine work provided the basis also for Sullivan's innovations in the field of
commercial architecture, and it is out of the Richardson-
Sullivan sphere that there emerged one of the founders of
modern architecture, Frank Lloyd Wright (1869–1959). In
the 1890s and early 1900s, Wright built a series of private
houses in Illinois in which primitivistic tendencies are fused
with revolutionary ideas in domestic planning. An early
admirer of Japanese architecture, Wright brought into
Middle West houses some of its proportions and its clear
but informal relationships, and combined them with traditional elements in American housing as well as his own
ideal of the articulated but undivided interior space.
Wright was a pioneer also of reinforced concrete architecture in the United States, at the same time as Auguste
Perret and others in Europe, but it was especially his domestic work that became influential in Europe from 1910,
when the first of a series of volumes illustrating his work
was published in Germany.

ART NOUVEAU DESIGN

The architectural side of the Art Nouveau movement drew
strength from picturesque primitivism as well as from the
increasing use of metal in buildings. The last time that
architecture, painting, sculpture and the applied arts had
worked together in one spirit had been in the Neo-Classical
period. Now for a time this unity was re-established, and

36. **Victor Horta.** *Maison Horta, Brussels, Dining-room.* 1895.
Architectural Art Nouveau appears to have sprung fully armed
from the head of this Belgian architect in 1892. This interior
shows his use of flowing vegetable lines for furniture and furnishings within a relatively geometrically structured room.

37, 38. **Charles Rennie Mackintosh.** *Glasgow Art School.*
Exterior (1898–1909) and *interior of Library* (1907–9). While he is
thought of as one of the finest designers in the Art Nouveau
movement, Mackintosh's talents ranged wider than that style
would suggest. The front of his School reveals his attachment to
asymmetrical masses of masonry, stressed by the linear hardness
of metal; the later Library shows him placing lines and planes
in space with a clarity that heralds the rise of the *De Stijl* movement ten years later.

there has continued to be much fruitful interchange between the arts. As principally a linear style, Art Nouveau
36 invited the use of metal for interiors (as in the work of Victor Horta, 1861–1947) and exteriors (as in the Paris Métro
stations designed around 1900 by Hector Guimard, (1867–
1942).

The art that scarcely benefitted at all from the new style
was sculpture, tied as it was to the representation of the
human figure. But in the hands of some architects, the Art
Nouveau period brought to a grand climax the partly
sculptural art of massing, and generally encouraged a
departure from the straight lines and right angles that are
normally considered the bases of architectural design. The
Spanish architect, Antonio Gaudi (1852–1926), is an extreme example of a man who took to its conclusion his age's
desire to work outside the old stylistic limits, turning Art
Nouveau into a subjective and almost expressionistic idiom
and giving his buildings the character of a hand-moulded
or vegetable form. Begun in 1884 and still fragmentary, but
45 built mostly in the 1890s, his Church of the Holy Family in
Barcelona is a masterly yet free exercise in the Gothic vein

in which Art Nouveau and the primitive building forms
that Gaudi had seen in Africa are brought together in a
structure that is in itself a masterpiece of rule-of-thumb and
craftsman's wiles. He was a man instinctively close to the
spirit of the medieval master masons; he worked for his
people and for the greater glory of God. His work continues
slowly but it has had no successors, though his admirers
have grown in number during the last twenty years or so.
In Glasgow, something of a similar spirit was driving
Charles Rennie Mackintosh (1869–1928) into designing
buildings and furniture that are as personal, as original as
Gaudi's, and, largely for historical reasons, more influential
on European developments. His Glasgow School of Art 37, 38
(1898 and 1907) wavers excitingly between simplicity or
functionalism (careful use of good materials, large and
plain windows to light the studios, the clear expression of
structural elements inside the main shell) and an element
of fantasy that smacks both of early nineteenth-century
Romanticism and the morbidity of *fin de siècle* art and
literature, expressed in over-weighty masses of masonry,
exaggerated structural gestures, and ironwork not so much
wrought as over-wrought. It is a building that stands between the picturesque tradition revived by Shaw and
Webb, the functionalism associated with European architecture of the 1920s and 1930s, and the urge towards constructional legibility particularly associated with the *De
Stijl* movement. In his own time Mackintosh's work, especially his furniture and interior designs, was of considerable
influence in other Art Nouveau centres, particularly in
Munich and Vienna.

The Twentieth Century: 1900-1920

The first decades of this century witnessed an extraordinarily rapid series of revolutionary movements in art and architecture, running parallel to dramatic developments in literature and music, in science and technology, and the whole political and social structure of the world. It was as though the great artists of the nineteenth century had prised open the floodgates and now a vast and varied sea of artistic creativity and inventiveness was let loose over mankind. Nineteenth-century painters had questioned the representational function of painting as well as conventions governing perspectival space, the modelling of figures set in that space, and even the need to approximate to the normal appearance of things. Now painters asserted the greatest possible freedom, not only departing much further from normal appearances of form and colour but rejecting the long tradition by which pictures were supposed to be based on facets of the visible world. At times they even abandoned the usual materials of painting, blurring the ancient demarcation between painting and sculpture. The sculptors of the later nineteenth century had weakened the hold of classicism and realism; now their successors were to challenge the whole concept of sculpture as the art of the tangible and the solid related to the world of objects in which we live, and investigated instead the interaction of planes and lines within the space in which they are set, or to invent forms which, even if they may embody some references to the visible world, are primarily independent of it and self-sufficient. In architecture, now that the way had been found out of the labyrinth of historicism, and some attempt been made to bring architecture and the rapidly progressing world of engineering together, new conceptions of design and building could be realised with great rapidity.

Each new movement brought with it its host of imitators and camp followers; each revolution produced its own academicism. The greatest masters are always too big to be contained in the movements with which they are associated, while to others the rebellious concepts that initiate a movement gradually become leaden conventions. The whole story of twentieth-century art is one of magnificent leaps forward and extraordinary regressions, of remarkable clear-sightedness on the part of a few protagonists and of misapprehension and thus devaluation on the part of many, of brilliant achievements and empty gestures, of profound originality and overflowing bandwagons. But, chaotic though it is, it is a story of unremitting vitality.

FAUVISM

The first of these revolutionary movements to come before the public was Fauvism. Henri Matisse (1869-1954) and a group of friends that included Derain, Vlaminck and 47 Rouault, contributed a roomful of pictures to a Paris exhibition in 1905 to find themselves labelled 'wild beasts' (*fauves*) and their work described as 'the barbaric and naïve splotches of a child playing with his box of colours'. Assertive and unnatural colour was certainly a characteristic of Fauvism, rooted in the lyrical Divisionism of Signac and

Cross, in Gauguin's decorative use of flat areas of unrepresentational colour, and in the vehement application of paint associated with van Gogh. Matisse was by far the greatest artist in the group. Aggressiveness was never part of his programme, though the paintings he did around 1905 include the most violent of his career. While some of his friends saw in the free use of form and colour a means of self-dramatisation, Matisse fused colour and form to convey his optical and emotional responses to his subject and constructed his paintings out of hard-won units of colour-form. 'What I dream of', he wrote in *Notes of a painter* (1908), 'is an art of balance, of purity and serenity'. Not a facilely agreeable art but one in which the outer and inner worlds are fused into a harmonious pictorial organisation. Between the outer world of objects and events, and the inner world of the artist's experience of these, he could see no conflict: his sensations belonged to both. To set down these sensations in an accurate and communicative way required the most delicate of adjustments: 'I want to reach that state of condensation of sensations which constitutes a picture'. Behind this lay not merely the subjectivism of Gauguin but also, significantly, the constructive spirit of Cézanne, as well as the long tradition of elegant painting in France: from the School of Fontainebleau, via Watteau, Boucher and Fragonard, to Renoir. Matisse devoted his art to such themes as beautiful women, interiors and flowers. The roughness that in about 1905 indicates a vein of rebelliousness (against Signac as well as against academic art) soon disappears from his work. Already in 1907 he has reached a point of balance: fluent lines that are pictorially so right that they seem more realistic than academic, colours that are often sharp and strange but are brought into unity—all of it energetic and taut but giving an impression of extraordinary peace. **46**

CUBISM

By this time, however, interest among Matisse's younger contemporaries was already moving away from Fauvism to an apparently more objective mode of painting. The death of Cézanne in 1906, followed by a retrospective exhibition in 1907, had drawn attention to his achievement as the creator of a new relationship between the picture and the objective world. The young Spaniard, Pablo Picasso (born 1881), had spent his youth in Barcelona where he and his friends looked to Art Nouveau as the gateway to a new, free and expressive art. After several visits to Paris, Picasso settled there in 1904. In his so-called Blue Period and Rose Period paintings (about 1901-5), he had evolved a personal idiom, largely traditional in character, capable of conveying melancholic and lyrical themes. Then, under the influence of Cézanne and of ancient Iberian carvings, Picasso turned to more fundamental problems of representation, abandoning a style that had begun to bring financial rewards. In the large and unfinished picture *Les Demoiselles d'Avignon* he demonstrated a new interest in monumentally constructed art. Large female nudes occupy **49**

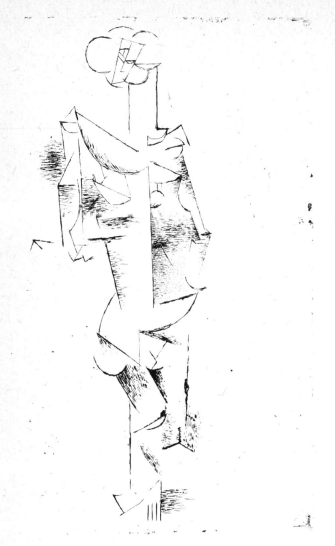

39. **Pablo Picasso.** *Mademoiselle Léonie.* 1910. Etching. Collection, The Museum of Modern Art, New York. Purchase. As Cubism became less concerned with sculptural mass and more with indicating the spatial context of objects, linear structure played a more and more decisive role. This can be seen in the paintings of 1910–11, but in a graphic work like this the formal devices invented by Picasso and Braque for this culmination of Analytical Cubism are shown most clearly.

lytical Cubist' phase, came in 1911, by which time Picasso and Braque had made their new idiom complete and in which year they produced some outstandingly beautiful demonstrations of it. In the same year a group of artists including Gleizes, Metzinger, Delaunay, Picabia, and Marcoussis, who may be described as second-string Cubists, exhibited together and thus brought Cubism before the public, and in 1912 Gleizes and Metzinger published a book on Cubism.

Although at the time it seemed that Cubism had finally removed all subjective elements from art and made the work of its practitioners indistinguishable (which had been said of Impressionism a generation earlier), the work of the Cubists varies greatly in character and significance. Some general points can be made. Analytical Cubism introduced and justified an artistic process that was at once destructive and recreative. The Cubists took a limited range of objects and destroyed their individual integrity: parts of a body mingle with parts of a table and parts of a bottle and a glass on that table. They abandoned the tradition of the single viewpoint, using several views of an object much as the Egyptians had drawn their figures to include conflicting but characteristic views, and thus they introduced an element of time or movement into their compositions, reemphasising the non-representational function of painting. The result is barely recognisable fifty years later. In so far as we do recognise the constituent objects, this is due to occasional hints in detail and to the reconstructive assembly of the parts in an arrangement that at times corresponds to the model as seen from various angles and that always aims at a pictorially coherent composition. The compositional arrangement in Analytical Cubism is normally quite traditional, focussing on the centre of the canvas and diminishing to the corners (a device that goes back at least to Leonardo da Vinci); at times they used an oval format to escape the problem of the empty corners. In terms of pictorial space, or composition in depth, they were

(Continued on page 97)

50

a shallow pictorial space closed by draperies. The swinging lines of the draperies and their sharp edges are echoed in the figures which only distantly relate to the normal forms of women and are almost devoid of modelling. The heads of the three women on the left have a primitiveness of form that relates to Iberian sculpture; those on the right are derived from African negro masks, long available in ethnological museums but only now being recognised for their artistic power. Georges Braque (1882–1963), a housepainter's son who had worked for a while with the Fauves, saw the *Demoiselles* in Picasso's studio in 1907. During the next four years he and Picasso worked closely together, evolving the dramatically new style known as Cubism. At first, in reaction against Fauvism, they ignored questions of colour and concentrated their research on form. What they sought was one element of Cézanne's intention: a way of capturing the three-dimensionality of things without destroying the two-dimensionality of the picture. Cézanne had approached this partly through colour. Picasso and Braque, after using the simplified solids they saw in African carvings and to which Cézanne had pointed in his famous dictum, 'Treat nature according to the cylinder, the sphere, the cone', with the result that some of their pictures were emphatically sculptural (quite unlike Cézanne's), found a new solution by breaking up the object before them into planes of simple form assembled in a shallow pictorial space. The climax of their work in this, the so-called 'Ana-

39

46. **Henri Matisse.** *Le Luxe II.* 1907–8. Casein. 82½ × 54¾ in. (209.5 × 139 cm.). Royal Museum of Fine Arts, Copenhagen. (Rump Collection). This is perhaps the earliest painting in which Matisse's sensitivity to line as a constructive and decorative element, and his unique control of broad colours are fully realised. It is probably no coincidence that Matisse and Picasso should have been working at lifesize figure subjects at much the same time. They may have been aware of each other's activities: they were certainly aware of the late figure paintings left by Cézanne (see plates 34 and 49). *Le Luxe II* is the second of two very similar paintings and is a marvellously refined version of the earlier work.

47. **Georges Rouault.** *The Old King.*
1936. Oil on canvas. 30¼ × 21¼ in.
(77 × 54 cm.). The Museum of Arts,
Carnegie Institute, Pittsburgh. Once one
of the most violently attacked of modern
painters, Rouault (1871–1958) was one
of the very few modern artists to use his
art as a vehicle for religious expression.
His paintings, with their glowing colours
and strong linear divisions, recall the
stained glass he handled as a young
apprentice; they are built up in many
layers of paint and often suggest the
hieratic severity of a Byzantine icon.

48. **Henri Rousseau.** *The Sleeping Gypsy.*
1897. Oil on canvas. 51 × 79 in. (129.5 ×
200.5 cm.). Collection, The Museum of
Modern Art, New York. (Gift of Mrs
Simon Guggenheim). Most famous of the
'primitive' painters recognised by modern
art history, and the first to be honoured
by avant-garde artists, Rousseau confronts
us with the question: how naive was he?
Was his rejection of the academic traditions of illusionistic realism (against which
his more obviously self-conscious contemporaries were struggling with less
success) totally instinctive? He had the
highest regard for academic skills; at the
same time he appears to have been aware
of his naivety as something worth preserving. *The Sleeping Gypsy* is one of his
most elegant works. Its hypnotic and
visionary character makes it an outstanding predecessor to the usually much
clumsier efforts of the Surrealists. The
guitar and vase, in their subtle distortion
and direct presentation, point towards
the first Cubist still lifes of Picasso.

49. (above). **Pablo Picasso.** *Demoiselles d'Avignon.* 1907. Oil on canvas. 96 × 92 in. (244 × 233.5 cm.). Collection, The Museum of Modern Art, New York. (Acquired through the Lillie P. Bliss Bequest). This large figure composition clearly marks a turning point in Picasso's career, inspired probably by Cézanne's late figure paintings. His original intention was to paint a scene of sailors and prostitutes, but all action and symbolical meaning disappeared as Picasso concerned himself more and more with problems of construction and expression. Out of this concern, Cubism was born. The two heads on the right were painted last and show Picasso's interest in African masks.

50. (opposite). **Georges Braque.** *The Portuguese.* 1911. Oil on canvas. 41¾ × 32 in. (116 × 81 cm.). Kunstmuseum, Basle. A particularly fine example of Analytical Cubism, showing the characteristic effect of open relief in this kind of painting and its tendency towards monochrome— although Braque, in what is perhaps a peculiarly French manner, includes very delicately varied hues in his narrow colour range as well as very pleasing brushwork. The introduction of lettering in various places adds to the spatial ambiguity of the picture while also stressing the relatively illusory quality of everything but the lettering.

51. **Juan Gris.** *Portrait of Picasso.* 1912.
Oil on canvas. 29¼ × 36¾ in. (74 × 93.5
cm.). Courtesy of the Art Institute,
Chicago. (Gift of Leigh B. Block). Gris's
Cubism was always more cerebral than
that of Picasso and Braque. In this early
painting he used an arbitrary but fixed
pattern of contradictory light and shadow
to unfold and to co-ordinate aspects of the
subject. As a method this derives from
Analytical Cubism, but Gris avoids some
of the shortcomings of that style through
his attachment to the kind of tightly controlled articulation of the whole picture
area that is found in the work of Seurat.

52. **Umberto Boccioni.** *Forces of a Street.*
1911. Oil on canvas. $31\frac{1}{2} \times 39$ in. (100 ×
180 cm.). Collection: Dr Hänggi, Basle.
Boccioni's painting and sculpture, during
his short period of Futurist activity, varies
considerably as he tries to achieve the
synthesis of physical and metaphysical
elements demanded by the movement's
programme. Here he fuses aspects of
Cubism with Impressionism to convey the
optical and emotional experience offered
by a city thoroughfare at night. This
painting was included in the Futurist
exhibition which opened in Paris on
February 5th, 1912, and subsequently
toured Europe.

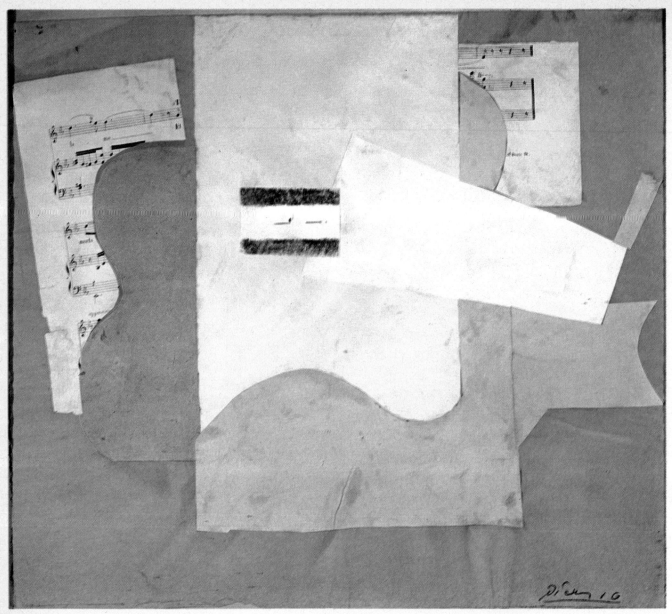

53, 54. **Pablo Picasso.** *Sheet of Music and Guitar.* 1912–13, (above). Gummed paper with pastel. $25\frac{1}{2} \times 23$ in. (65×58 cm.). Collection: Georges Salles, Paris. *Mandolin.* 1914, (below). Wood construction. $23\frac{1}{2}$ in. (60 cm.) high. Artist's collection. In his Synthetic Cubist work Picasso abandoned the painterly and illusionist aspects of Analytical Cubism and treated the canvas or board on which he was working as a support on which to construct images. Often he used pieces of paper and other materials that involved some degree of projection from this support, and a logical extension of this was the constructed relief. Picasso produced a series of such reliefs in 1913–14 and these inspired the development of Constructivist sculpture in Russia.

55. **Umberto Boccioni.** *Muscular Dynamism* or *Unique forms of Continuity in Space.* 1913. Polished bronze. $43\frac{1}{2}$ in. high. (110.5 cm.). Museum of Modern Art, Milan. In this study of a figure in motion, Boccioni turned away from the photographic records of movements that fascinated some of his friends, (particularly Ballà), to find a formal means of giving sensations of movement. The result is oddly similar to the effects of the fluttering draperies of Baroque sculpture, and particularly to that Hellenistic figure, the *Victory of Samothrace,* specifically denigrated in Marinetti's first Futurist Manifesto of 1909 in favour of the new beauty of a racing car.

56. **Robert Delaunay.** *Circular Forms.* 1912. Oil on canvas. $50\frac{7}{8} \times 50\frac{7}{8}$ in. (129.2 × 129.2 cm.). The Solomon R. Guggenheim Museum, New York. Delaunay's concentration on the expressive power of interacting colours remains one of the most influential acts of 20th-century art. Though not absolutely unique (Kandinsky in Germany, Kupka in France, Ballà in Italy were moving in much the same direction about the same time), Delaunay's abstract colour compositions today look the least dated and have been the most fruitful. Here painting approaches most nearly to the condition of music.

57. **Marc Chagall.** *Self-portrait with Seven Fingers.* 1911. Oil on canvas. 42 × 50½ in. (107 × 128 cm.). Stedelijk Museum, Amsterdam. (Collection: Regnault). Marc Chagall was born in Vitebsk, Russia, in 1889. He spent 1910–14 in Paris, returned to Russia for the years 1914–22. Since then he has lived almost continuously in France. During his first years in Paris he became acquainted with the Cubists and was influenced by their disruptive transformation of visual appearances. But his art is characterised by a lyrical expressionism in which the painter reveals his experiences and dreams, and in which his Russian-Jewish origin is represented through its vigorous folklore culture and its rich vein of poetry. This picture shows both the influence of Cubism and the all-pervading element of fantasy peculiar to Chagall.

58. **Fernand Léger.** *The Acrobats.* 1918. Oil on canvas. 38 × 46 in. (97 × 117 cm.). Kunstmuseum, Basle. As a socialist, Léger evolved out of Synthetic Cubism a language of painting that would, he hoped, bring art into the world of the proletariat's labour and leisure. Strong and clearly defined forms, suggesting machinery, are presented in energetic colours that bring a note of gaiety and optimism to a world more usually associated with smoke and grease. So Léger does not represent the miseries of the working class, but uses his art to celebrate the world of labour as virile and vigorous.

59. **Ernst Ludwig Kirchner.** *Reclining Nude with Fan.* 1908. Oil on cloth. 25¼ × 36¼ in. (64 × 92 cm.). Kunsthalle, Bremen. Kirchner was the most gifted of the *Brücke* painters. By bringing technical brashness and a personal note of emotion into his representation of unexceptional subjects, he hoped to give new life to an art that seemed to him suffocated by academic values and enfeebled by stylistic in-breeding.

60. **Oskar Kokoschka.** *Still-life with Sheep and Hyacinth.* 1909. Oil on canvas. 34¼ × 45 in. (87 × 114 cm.). Öster-reichische Galerie, Vienna. Oskar Kokoschka (born 1886) was of Czech and Austrian parentage and grew up in Vienna, where, as a young man, he became known as a particularly vehement and revolutionary painter and playwright. Viennese painting had sunk to a low level during the nineteenth century and had then blossomed luxuriantly in the Art Nouveau years around 1900. Kokoschka was one of those who rejected the artificiality of Art Nouveau and placed great emphasis on the closeness of art to everyday life, its tensions and conflicts as well as its beauty.

61. **Wassily Kandinsky.** *Bright Picture.* 1913. Oil on canvas. 30¾ × 39½ in. (78 × 100 cm.). The Solomon R. Guggenheim Museum, New York. This is one of Kandinsky's earliest completely abstract oil paintings, and probably one of the most entirely spontaneous. Kandinsky's Abstract Expressionism offered a funda-mentally new means of presenting emotions and sensations in pictorial form, short-cutting the process, illustrated by Kirchner and Kokoschka, of transmitting them through recognisable subject-matter. Kandinsky showed that the picture can function as a surface on which the artist expresses himself directly through physical gestures, recorded by means of the brushes and paints that are an extension of himself.

62. **Franz Marc.** *Fighting Forms.* 1914.
Oil. $35\frac{3}{4} \times 51\frac{1}{2}$ in. (91×130 cm.).
Bayerische Staatsgemäldesammlungen,
Munich. Some of his last works show this
German painter, member of the *Blaue
Reiter* group in Munich, moving from a
somewhat sentimental nature-worshipping
modernised realism to an exploration of
abstract form that owes much to Futurism.

63. **Kasimir Malevich.** *Black Trapezium
and Red Square.* 1915. Oil on canvas.
$39\frac{3}{4} \times 24\frac{1}{2}$ in. (101.5×62 cm.). Stedelijk
Museum, Amsterdam. Malevich was the
first painter to explore the optical and
communicative properties of simple
shapes, beginning with the black square
and then going on to more complicated
relationships.

64. (opposite). **Marcel Duchamp.** *The
Large Glass* or *Bride Stripped Bare by her
Bachelors Even.* 1915–28. Oil and lead wire
on glass (in two parts). $109\frac{1}{4} \times 69$ in.
(277.5×175.5 cm.). Philadelphia
Museum of Art. (Louise & Walter
Arensberg Collection). One of the great
milestones of modern art, and in many
respects the most radical and revolutionary work of its generation.

65. **Constantin Brancusi.** *The Fish.*
1930. Grey marble (fish). Stone (base).
21 × 71 in. (53.5 × 180.5 cm.), (fish).
28½ in. (72.5 cm.), (base). Collection,
The Museum of Modern Art, New York.
(Acquired through the Lillie B. Bliss
Bequest). Like Michelangelo, Brancusi
felt that carving was concerned with
finding the ideal form within the stone. In
rejecting the Renaissance and 19th-
century concentration on the figure, he
sought an original independent image
that the material and the instinctive
direction of the artist would allow to
emerge. This image could have an
accidental resemblance to things in
nature; the title could be used to
accentuate this.

66. **Umberto Boccioni.** *Development of a
Bottle in Space.* 1912. Silver-plated bronze.
15 in. (38 cm.), high. Collection, The
Museum of Modern Art, New York.
(Aristide Maillol Fund). This work, by
the finest futurist artist, appears to relate
more directly to Cubism than to the
complexities of Futurism. The bottle is
intuitively dissected to reveal its structure;
the energies that appear to come from it
are given solid form. Comparable
instances of dissection and objectification
can be seen in the painting of Juan Gris.

profoundly original. Having followed the example of the Post-Impressionists in reducing the space that seems to exist behind the canvas, the Cubists at times appeared to project some of their facets forward to penetrate the real space in front of the canvas—illusionism turned inside out. Coming after Fauvism, Cubism at the time appeared a harsh and disciplined manner of painting. Today it is clear that its basis was subjective and sensational.

FUTURISM

Meanwhile, a related movement had come into existence in Italy and was about to erupt on the Paris art scene. The poet, Marinetti, had gathered around himself a group of young artists to propagate and demonstrate the heady joys of Futurism. This meant an enthusiastic acceptance of the modern technological world: machines, mass-production, mechanical sounds, speed, the destruction of everything old. 'We will sing of the stirring of great crowds—workers, pleasure-seekers, rioteers—and the confused sea of colour and sound as revolution sweeps through a modern metropolis. We will sing the midnight fervour of arsenals and shipyards blazing with electric moons; insatiable stations swallowing the smoking serpents of their trains, factories hung from the clouds by the twisted threads of their smoke...' (from Marinetti's *Futurist Manifesto*, published in *Le Figaro*, Paris, on February 20, 1909). The chief value of this new romanticism was that it related to the present, to physical and spiritual experiences that could be shared by everyone who travelled on a tram or merely opened his window on the bustle of a modern city. The aggressiveness of Futurism was a product partly of youth and partly of the great weight of the classical tradition that pressed on the shoulders of any Italian attempting to drag his country out of the artistic slough into which it had sunk since the days of Tiepolo. The *Manifesto of the Futurist Painters* (February 11, 1910) repeatedly asserted their rejection of the entire past and their support for originality and audacity. The *Technical Manifesto of Futurist Painting* (April 11, 1910) went some way towards defining how these attitudes were to affect their work. Above all, they were to accept the reality of movement as opposed to the artificial or unusual condition of stillness, and, a corollary of this, the interaction and mutual interpenetration of the things around us in our experience. 'Painters have always shown us things and persons in front of us. We shall place the spectator at the centre of the picture'.

To realise these conceptions in art was not so easy as to define them. The Futurists, for all their bravado, knew they must look to Paris for guidance as well as for a platform from which to address the world of art. This guidance they found first in Divisionism and then in Cubism. As techniques, both are suited to indicating the mutual interpenetration of things, and Cubism, by its references to objects as seen from differing viewpoints, could imply both the movement of the object and that of the painter and the spectator. But for more compelling images of movement

and speed the Futurists turned to the camera. From photographers' studies they learned how movement could be indicated by a repetition of objects, or of the most mobile parts of objects, and even by abstracted lines (akin to those 'shock waves' we know from photographs of models in windtunnels) that could suggest movement and also the response to that movement of the object's environment.

The most important artists in the movement were Boccioni, Severini, Carrà and Balla. Umberto Boccioni **55, 66** (1882–1916) was certainly the most creative amongst them, and his picture *Forces of a Street* (1911) is one of the most **52** complete and successful demonstrations of their ideas. Reference has been made already to the complex of sensations woven by Turner into his late paintings. The same words could be used of this Futurist painting, but the basic difference is that whereas Turner was concerned with timeless and more or less universal experiences known to anyone alive to the forces of nature, the Futurists deal with the particularities of urban society at the beginning of this century and to some extent even with the particular social and urban conditions obtaining in Northern Italy at this time. Stylistically, they contributed little to painting, but their insistence on the dynamism of life as a basis for art permanently affected modern aesthetics. We shall refer in due course to Futurism's part in the development of sculpture and architecture. The movement's immediate success was considerable. In February, 1912, they had their first group exhibition in Paris, and from Paris the exhibition (and some of the artists) went on to London, Berlin, Brussels, Hamburg, Amsterdam, The Hague, Munich, Vienna, Budapest, Breslau, Frankfurt, Wiesbaden, Zürich and Dresden. Publications and lectures spread their ideas even further afield.

SYNTHETIC CUBISM

The immediate consequence of the Futurist exhibition in Paris appears to have been that of giving renewed impetus to Cubism. Delaunay and the other second-string Cubists were encouraged by the Italians' example in their move away from the almost monochromatic and pseudo-scientific character of Analytical Cubism. Picasso and Braque, who were not impressed by the noisy upstarts from Milan, moved during 1912 from the Analytical phase of Cubism into what is known as the Synthetic phase—a change **53, 54** which involved a substantially different attitude to reality and to the materials of art as well as a surprisingly ironical view of art as such. While Analytical Cubism was concerned with a process of destroying the object and reconstructing it as a pictorial composition in what appears to be a shallow pictorial space, Synthetic Cubism usually involved the construction of objects (with paint or other materials) effectively on the canvas. Early in 1912, Picasso used a piece of oil cloth in a picture and so initiated collage; in September Braque stuck on his canvas pieces of wallpaper printed to resemble wood. These acts refuted the tradition of skilful paint-handling which had contributed greatly to the beauty of many Analytical Cubist works; they also, by bringing bits of the real world into the artificial world of the picture, indicated a kind of double-take on the issue of what is fact and what is fiction, and this could become a triple-take, as when Braque began to paint sections of pictures to look like pieces of wallpaper. Soon other materials (matchboxes, corrugated cardboard), technical devices (decorator's comb, normally used for wood graining), and textures both physical (sand in paint) and optical (dotted and striped areas) were brought into Synthetic Cubism, and with all these came a new interest in colour. The new works of Braque and Picasso often seem to have been assembled on the canvas rather than painted, and project forward from the canvas even when no extraneous materials are used. From the use of materials and textures that normally have specific contexts or meanings there resulted a double function that has remained of great importance in modern art (and thence in advertising design, etc.): pictures could be planned as abstract organisations, often of quite large units, and yet at the same time the shape and/or the particular character of the collage materials (or imitation collage) could be used to indicate specific subject-matter. By 1913 Picasso was producing reliefs based on these ideas, as well as paintings.

In 1911 Picasso and Braque had been joined by the Spaniard, Juan Gris (1887–1927). More intellectual and analytical than they, Gris became the theoretician of Synthetic Cubism, the writer who could link Cubism to contemporary developments in science, as well as the painter of some exceptionally clearly organised pictures. His work is normally based on a firm geometrical structure which Gris gradually particularised to indicate certain objects; he said he did not wish spectators to read their own interpretations into his pictures. Robert Delaunay (1885–1941) meanwhile moved from a series of pictures which he called *Windows*, almost completely abstracted and richly coloured works in which hints of townscape come through a soft chequered pattern that may have been suggested by lace curtains but can also be seen as a regularised version of Divisionism, into completely abstract paintings, which 56 he called *Disks* (begun late 1912) and in which colour, arranged in segmental shapes, produces a rhythmic surging and swaying. Delaunay was probably not the first artist to produce completely abstract work in which no reference to any particular part of the visible world is intended, but he was the first to give full reign to the optical and emotive power of colour.

EXPRESSIONISM IN GERMANY

Although Delaunay's work was hailed by the poet-critic Apollinaire and was shown in Paris, it made a far greater impression in Germany. There the early years of the century had seen the eruption of one of the movements and ͏ activities that are assembled under the general ͏ ression. In Dresden in 1905, a handful of young ͏ se studies had been principally architectural,

formed themselves into a revolutionary group of painters. They called themselves *Die Brücke* (The Bridge) to indicate their desire to form a link between all revolutionary tendencies in art. They did not, that is, propose particular theories or styles other than those associated with anti-academicism. In some respects the character of their work comes close to that of the Fauves, without, it seems, their having had much knowledge of the French group: their colours are vehement, their brushwork is often brusque, and their design shows affinities with primitive art. But while a lot of Fauve painting aimed at ultimately decorative qualities of harmony and rhythm, and thus can be seen as an extension of Gauguin's achievement, Expressionism in general and the *Brücke* painters especially aimed at intense and particular communication. Whereas Fauvism, for all its apparent wildness, can be seen as essentially a part of the French tradition of fine painting, Expressionism represents a resurgence of Nordic anguish and pessimism, sharpened by the disturbed condition of German society at the time, and linked artistically to the bitter and emotional art of such earlier Northerners as Munch and Ensor, to some aspects of German early Romanticism, and to German art of the time of the Reformation, before classicism had imposed its veneer of dignity. From the art of Grünewald and his contemporaries the *Brücke* painters learnt the value of figural distortion, and to this they joined an intensification of the brushwork until it took on gestural qualities. One of the group's most successful ventures was the revitalisation of graphic art. Helped by the example of Munch and Gauguin, but inspired mainly by their pre-

40. **Karl Schmidt-Rottluff.** *Road to Emmaus.* 1918. Woodcut. $15\frac{1}{2} \times 19\frac{1}{2}$ in. (39 × 50 cm.). Philadelphia Museum of Art. The artists of *Die Brücke* brought new vigour to the long tradition of German graphic art, under the influence both of Munch and Gauguin and of primitive art.

41. **Paul Klee.** *Drawing with the Fermata.*
1918. Ink on paper. 6¼ × 9½ in.
(16 × 24.5 cm.). Klee Foundation,
Berne. Klee moved freely between
figuration and abstraction. In many
pictures and drawings he reveals a special
interest in the aesthetic and communicative function of signs and symbols. It is
possible that (as this example may be
taken to suggest) his musicianship may
have inspired this interest.

decessors of about 1500, they produced a great deal of graphic art of considerable power and originality, and generally encouraged the German public to take a more serious interest in graphic work than has been the case in other countries. Around 1910, the *Brücke* artists moved to Berlin. In 1913, recognising their growing diversity, they dissolved the group.

By that time another group had been formed in Munich. Its protagonist was the Russian, Wassily Kandinsky (1866–1944), who had arrived in the Bavarian capital to study art at the age of thirty. He was deeply affected by the current Art Nouveau movement which he fused with Russian folklore elements, and then, influenced by Fauvism and by the folk art of southern Bavaria, turned to a free and sono-rous style of landscape painting. More and more compelled by colour, Kandinsky in 1910 produced an abstract watercolour painting, a spontaneous expression in coloured marks on paper of the pressing emotions of a moment. During the next seven or eight years he developed this kind 61 of free abstraction, now known as Abstract Expressionism, allowing references to his favourite themes (landscape, horsemen, etc.) to show among more or less abstract con-figurations, sometimes working impetuously and some-times building up larger and more considered compositions on the basis of a series of sketches. In 1912 he published a book *Concerning the spiritual in art* in which he argued for the inner world of man as the true source of artistic creation, and for 'inner necessity' as art's driving force and subject. In the same year, he and his friend, Franz Marc (1880–1916), produced a volume of essays by various writers with 62 illustrations of old and new art called *Der Blaue Reiter* (The Blue Rider), which was the name also of a group that they and their friends had started in 1911. Like *Die Brücke*, *Der Blaue Reiter* proposed no specific dogma or style, but whereas the Dresden group consisted of a handful of young Germans making a protest that was as much social as artistic against the world around them, the Munich group,

international in its membership and affiliations, looked only for new and more richly expressive languages of art. Theirs was a more meditative and constructive expression-ism, an attempt to move art away from the world of fact into the world of the spirit, and, partly owing to Kandins-ky's own inclinations, they recognised colour as their most powerful weapon. Delaunay was a considerable influence on the group. He and other French, Swiss and Russian artists contributed to *Blaue Reiter* exhibitions, and from Munich these exhibitions were sent out over Germany. The 1914–18 war destroyed the group by dispersing its members and claiming some of them as its victims.

The artist who, while only loosely connected with *Der Blaue Reiter*, continued to work in its spirit and develop some of its ideas, was Paul Klee (1879–1940). Ever since he 41, 75 started to study art in Munich in 1898, Klee had been 81 searching for the essential art of painting. In his drawing he early achieved complete individuality and control—a con-trol as much of the spirit as of the hand—but for more than a decade he worked his way towards an equal command of painting. Colour, he knew, was the basic issue, and he worked incessantly to acquire an instinctive knowledge of colour, comparable to the pianist's knowledge of the sounds he can produce through his keyboard. He made continual technical and aesthetic experiments, studied the work of other artists, especially Cézanne. In 1914, he visited North Africa where, more profoundly even than Delacroix about eighty years earlier, he was deeply stirred by the colour and calm exoticism of the environment, and found himself at last a colourist and thus a painter. From that time on Klee drew and painted with incredible fluency and inventive-ness. For him art was something that emerged almost accidentally out of an interaction of the artist's intellect and subconscious with the technical means and skills at his command. 'Let everything grow' is the root principle of all his thought: out of the recognition of the potentialities of the simplest motifs, sparingly used, can come works are filled with the human spirit and echo nature's creative processes. He saw no conflict between abstraction and figuration, and though several movements claimed him as a fellow worker he never belonged to any.

REVOLUTIONARY PAINTING IN RUSSIA

Kandinsky, returning to Moscow in 1914, found there an art world as well as a political world bubbling with revolution. For some years Moscow had kept itself closely informed on what was going on in Western Europe. The educated Muscovite probably knew more about the European avant-garde than his equal in Paris. Fauvism, Cubism and Futurism were known about almost as soon as they happened, and contact between Moscow and German art centres (especially Munich) was particularly close.

Out of a number of avant-garde actions that of Kasimir 63 Malevich (1878–1935) was the most decisive and has become almost legendary. 'When in 1913', he wrote later, 'in a desperate attempt to rid art of the ballast of objectivity, I took refuge in the form of the square, and exhibited a picture that represented nothing more than a black square on a white field, the critics—and with them society—sighed, "All that we loved has been lost. We are in a desert. Before us stands a black square on a white ground".... But the desert is filled with the spirit of non-objective feeling, which penetrates everything.' In 1913–14, under the influence of Paris, Malevich had developed a personal fusion of Synthetic Cubism with Futurism, but this he rejected in favour of something less arbitrary (he did not actually exhibit his black square until 1915, but a backdrop he designed in 1913 came close to it). One is tempted to see the Russian tradition of the icon behind his elevation of a basic geometrical form to art status, but what struck his contemporaries was the heroically austere gesture of excluding all ingratiating factors, of subject-matter, brushwork, perspective and even colour, from his picture. It was easily the most ruthless gesture any artist had made. At the same time, it was also one of the most constructive. It focussed attention on the optical and affective properties of a black square on a white ground, that is, on the particular expression of a square of a certain size and blackness in a particular relationship with a larger white square (to be exact, only a white margin: here we meet one aspect of the figure-field ambiguities discussed by Gestalt psychologists and exploited by many later painters). This made possible a revaluation of the most fundamental and apparently most simple ingredients of art and has led to some of the strongest works of our century. Having said this, we must add that a painter like Matisse, simplifying form and colour to the most telling and unconventional relationships, or ... Klee, half playfully testing the potentialities of linear ... tches of colour, was similarly discharging ... le custom and over-use. What links these ..., like Kandinsky and Delaunay, is a new ... d regard for the power of 'a flat surface ... lours assembled in a certain order' (to refer

back to Denis's challenging statement of 1890) to affect us directly through our sensations.

Malevich soon went on to more complex assemblies of form and colour. After the Revolution of 1917, he and his friends were given positions of power in Russian art and education. Kandinsky, for example, was for a time in charge of an Institute of Artistic Culture which, he hoped, would systematically investigate the properties of the grammar of art. Malevich's movement, which he called Suprematism ('By Suprematism I mean the primacy of pure sensation in the visual arts'), attracted many followers for a time and was closely related to a sculptural movement that later became known as Constructivism. But dissensions between the artists and, after 1920, the rejection by Lenin and his government of any art that did not obviously serve industry and propaganda, put an end to progressive art in Russia.

HOLLAND: DE STIJL

In Holland, however, a similar movement had come into being. During the war years, Piet Mondrian (1872–1944), 67 earlier a hypersensitive painter of landscape, had developed Analytical Cubism into a personal idiom of great beauty, and had then gradually simplified that idiom until he was painting seascapes consisting of nothing but neat vertical and horizontal strokes of black paint on white. At this moment (1917), he met Theo van Doesburg (1883–1931). They formed the *De Stijl* (the style) group and published a magazine of the same name. Under Mondrian's aesthetic leadership, the group propagated an art of dynamic balance in which a few basic elements—vertical and horizontal black bands and rectangular areas of primary colours, white or grey—would be composed without reference to the visible world. Theirs was to be an art of pure spiritual beauty that would offer examples of harmony and stability formed of contrasts to a world suffering from extremes of uniformity and conflict. In the 1920s the internal development and external influence of *De Stijl* were to be of great importance.

ART ATTACKS ART: DADA

More characteristic of the war years and of the period immediately following the war were those to whom the bloodshed and misery of the age seemed to confirm the bankruptcy of western civilisation and who made it their business to advertise this bankruptcy by mocking the culture on which the West had prided itself. Like Rousseau they denied the sanity of reason, but whereas Rousseau had pointed to man's dreams of beauty and his sensibility before nature as sources of regeneration, they opposed unreason to reason and anti-art to art. Such men were to be found throughout Europe and also, more rarely, in the United States. In Switzerland, a neutral oasis in a sea of violence, an international group came together and propagated such ideas. In 1916, a handful of émigrés met in Zürich and founded the Cabaret Voltaire—Germans, a Rumanian, a

42. **Robert Wiene** (director). *Still from the film 'The Cabinet of Dr Caligari'.* Germany, 1919. This film was conceived by its authors as a 'condemnation of insane authority', and is characteristic of the rebellious spirit in Germany after the disasters inflicted by the government on the people in the first world war. The décor was the work of Walter Reimann, Walter Rohrig and Hermann Warm, all associated with that focal organisation of German Expressionism, the gallery *Der Sturm* and its journal.

Hungarian, and Jean (or Hans) Arp who, having been born in Alsace-Lorraine (in 1887), was of variable nationality. There they wrote poetry, made objects, and presented wild cabaret performances, all to satirise art and literature. They called themselves 'Dada', the most significantly meaningless name they could find, yet one that is the beginning of all speech. Paradoxically, they proved only that anti-art cannot be. Their literary nonsense had a liberating effect on writing, breaking through limitations of syntax and normal discourse; in art, their exploitation of accidental effect and alogical relationships revealed possibilities only vaguely glimpsed before and which many have been willing to explore and use since. The French artist, Marcel Duchamp (born 1887), who had been one of the fringe Cubists in 1911–12, and who from 1915 onwards lived almost continuously in the United States, was certainly the finest embodiment of Dada ideas although he was never a member of the group. One of the most inventive forces in modern art, he was also, speaking numerically, one of the least productive. In a long life he has created only a small body of work, but practically every one is a masterpiece. The greatest of them is the so-called *Large Glass* on which he worked for eight years (1915–23), the summation and apotheosis of his work and thought up to that time. It was laboriously painted and otherwise deposited on two sheets of glass which were accidentally broken in 1926; characteristically, Duchamp accepted the cracks, which now are seen as an integral part of the design, as a sympathetic contribution from fate.

The Dada vein in modern art, it should be noted, is unique. The Renaissance produced works of a minor kind, like Arcimboldo's vegetable heads, which were considered entertaining and skilful, and in the world of caricature there are things that could be thought of as mocking art. But it is characteristic of our century alone that much of the art produced in it should directly and indirectly question the function and the value of art. For while Dada raised these questions, publicly they were implicit in most avant-garde developments of these decades, and the works in which they are raised often stand far outside what had been thought of as the realm of art. The aggrandisement of this realm during the period 1900–1920 is quite unprecedented in extent and speed; in subsequent decades artists have on the whole been satisfied to develop and fructify portions of the newly-won terrain.

DEVELOPMENTS IN SCULPTURE

This is as true of sculpture as of painting. In 1900, for all the achievements of Rodin and Rosso, sculpture was still a very circumscribed field. The most important sculpture produced during the first two decades of this century represents both extensions of the freedom won by them—one thinks of Matisse's free and vital handling of clay and the human form—and the rejection of their tradition in order to explore new fields. Once the value of African carvings and of primitive sculpture generally had been realised by the painters, the sculptors, too, found themselves confronted by alternative and unexplored traditions, and a great deal of the work of this period reveals the firm organisation and simplified forms of primitive prototypes. But among the African pieces admired at this time there were also constructed (as opposed to carved) works, and these, in combination with the example set by two-dimensional and low relief Synthetic Cubism, may have contributed to

64

28

43, 44, 45. **Henri Matisse.** *Jeannette, I (Jeanne Vaderin*, 1st state, above). 1910. Bronze. 13 in. high (33 cm.). Collection, The Museum of Modern Art, New York (acquired through the Lillie P. Bliss Bequest). *Jeannette, II (Jeanne Vaderin*, 2nd state, above, right). 1910. Bronze. 10⅜ in. high (26.5 cm.). Collection, The Museum of Modern Art, New York (Gift of Sidney Janis). *Jeannette, V (Jeanne Vaderin*, 5th state, right). 1910–11? Bronze. 22⅞ in. (58 cm.). Collection, The Museum of Modern Art, New York (acquired through the Lillie P. Bliss Bequest). Matisse produced a considerable body of sculpture, most of it between 1900 and 1930. In this series of heads we see him developing the form in the same way as it tends to develop in his drawing: from a delicate and vivid representation of the subject to a decisively transformed arabesque that fuses the character of the subject with a powerful abstract image.

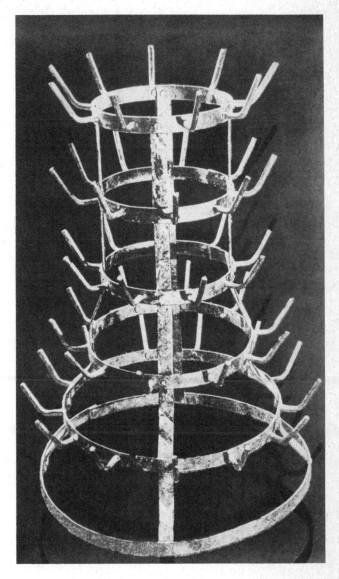

46. **Vladimir Tatlin.** *Relief.* 1917. Wood, zinc sprayed on iron.
39½ × 25¼ in. (100 × 64 cm.). Tretyakov Gallery, Moscow.
That key discovery of Cubism, the work of art as an assembled
or constructed object, found its development first at the hands
of the Russian Constructivists, of whom Tatlin appears to have
been the first.

47. **Marcel Duchamp.** *Bottlerack.* 1914. Galvanised iron,
ready-made. 23¼ × 14½ in. at its base (59 × 37 cm.). Original
lost; replica, Man Ray, Paris. One logical extension of intro-
ducing 'real' materials into art, such as a sheet of newspaper to
represent a newspaper, can be that of omitting the art (in the
sense of something created by the artist) altogether.

emergence of a completely new kind of sculpture that is
assembled out of separate pieces of material, rather than
modelled or carved, and often eschews the traditional
solidity of sculpture. This kind of sculpture was already
hinted at in the disintegration of objects into an open relationship of planar facets shown in Analytical Cubism, and
one may with some justice relate interests of this kind to the
contemporary redefinitions of matter and time-space proposed by men on the frontiers of science. Within sculpture
itself a very important contribution was that of Boccioni,
who on April 11, 1912, published a *Technical Manifesto of
Futurist Sculpture*, that demanded and described radically
new kinds of sculpture as well as rejecting the old. He
55 wanted sculpture of energy, of space, of relationships, that
would be made of all sorts of materials, and could be
mechanically mobile. Most of his sculpture, which included various experiments on this basis, has been destroyed.

The fuller realisation of some of these ideas was achieved
in Russia. Vladimir Tatlin (1885–1953), who visited *46*
Picasso in 1913, returned home to begin a series of constructed sculptures made of whatever materials came to
hand. During the war years other artists, like the brothers
Antoine Pevsner (1886–1962) and Naum Gabo (born *62, 63*
1890) joined what became known as the 'Constructivist'
movement. In 1920 their *Realistic Manifesto* insisted that
'Space and time are the two elements which exclusively fill
real life', and they went on to develop personal and poetic
modes of Constructivism.

Marcel Duchamp meanwhile confronted the world with
two apparently off-hand works of lasting significance. In
1913 he fastened a bicycle wheel to a stool and presented it
as the first mobile sculpture. In 1914 he elected a normal
French galvanised metal bottle-rack to become a work of
art, and subsequently presented other such 'ready-made'
Synthetic Cubism had shown that art could be ma

48. Jacques Duchamp-Villon. *The Horse.* 1914. Bronze. 40 in. high (101.5 cm.). Collection, The Museum of Modern Art, New York (Van Gogh Purchase Fund). One of the most forceful of early Cubo-Futurist sculptures, Duchamp-Villon's *Horse* shows the abstracted forms and that sense of pounding energy proposed by these movements while referring ambiguously to animal and engine forms.

49. Alexander Archipenko. *Seated Figure.* 1916. Terracotta. 21¾ in. (55 cm.). Kunstmuseum, Düsseldorf. Archipenko learnt from Cubism the juxtaposing of positive and negative forms and generally gave his sculptures forms of an inorganic and mechanistic kind.

found objects; Duchamp showed that found objects could be art, implying that anything is art if the artist wills it so and that art resides not in the making of the art work but in the recognition of an object's aesthetic value. Arp brought into sculpture the Dada concept of chance as a creative force, making reliefs in which the disposition of the forms was based on unplanned relationships and unexpected hints of meaning.

BRANCUSI AND OTHER SCULPTORS

At the other end of the artistic spectrum stood a sculptor, remote from all movements and manifestos, in whose work both the vigour and the refinement of modern art find their fullest expression. Constantin Brancusi (1876–1957) came to Paris from his native Rumania in 1904, was deeply affected by the example of Rodin and Rosso, and then turned from both to find his own way. He developed two very different styles. On the one hand, he carved (and sometimes modelled) exquisitely refined forms that seem to embody absolutes of perfection while at the same time confronting us as physically provocative and magnetic presences. These were far removed from the fleshy charms of so much traditional sculpture (to which Brancusi referred as 'beefsteak'), but they were not total abstractions either, and they hold a unique balance between the world of the senses and the world of the ideal. On the other hand, he produced a series of rough, tough sculptures, carved from old pieces of wood, in which suggestions from the African carvings he found

50. **Georges Vantongerloo.** *Rapport des Volumes.* 1919. Stone. $4\frac{3}{4} \times 4\frac{3}{4} \times 7$ in. ($12 \times 12 \times 18$ cm.). Marlborough Fine Arts Gallery, London. Vantongerloo's first *De Stijl* sculptures investigate the formal relationship of void to mass within a precise volume—here a 12-centimetre cube, in other cases a sphere. Later he opened his sculpture out further, locating Neo-Plasticist elements so as to bring space into aesthetic contribution.

51. **Wilhelm Lehmbruck** (1881–1919).
Kneeling Woman. 1911. Cast stone. 69½ in.
high (176.5 cm.). Collection, The
Museum of Modern Art, New York (Gift
of Abby Aldrich Rockefeller). The best
known of German Expressionist sculptors,
Lehmbruck brings Gothic grace and
slimness to a kind of sculpture that marks
the last flickering of the classical tradition.

52. **Karl Schmidt-Rottluff.** *Head.* 1917.
Wood. 13½ in. high (34.5 cm.). Repro-
duced by courtesy of the Trustees of the
Tate Gallery, London. Most of the *Brücke*
painters produced occasional sculptures.
This head is one of a series done by
Schmidt-Rottluff under the influence of
African sculpture.

53. **Auguste Perret.** *Musée des Travaux
Publics.* Begun 1937. Reinforced concrete.
Perret used the versatile new material,
reinforced concrete, to extend the long
French tradition of sophisticated classicism. In some of his buildings he achieved
an elegance of design and technical refinement comparable only to French
work of the eighteenth century.

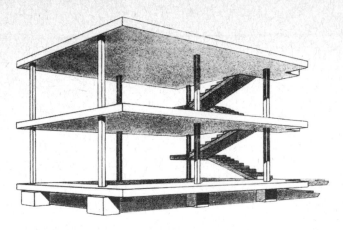

54. **Le Corbusier.** *Dom-Ino House constructional system.* 1914–15. In this diagram, the young Le Corbusier demonstrated the structural skeleton of a reinforced concrete house; internal divisions and external cladding could be varied and variable since they play no structural role.

being admired in Paris mingled with an innate primitivism linked to his peasant origins. These powerful and dramatic works complement his more meditative productions like the gargoyles of Gothic cathedrals that thrust themselves over the heads of the smiling saints below. Brancusi evolved his mature idioms at the time when Picasso and Braque were creating Analytical Cubism, opposing to their disruptive treatment of reality works of transcendant beauty that were more akin in spirit to the finest achievements of Matisse. He said: 'Do not look for strange formulas or mysteries. I offer you pure joy'. And added: 'Look at my sculptures until you manage to see them.'

More directly linked to developments in Cubism and Futurism were such sculptors as Laurens and Lipchitz, and the Russian-born Parisian, Alexander Archipenko (1887–1964), who made the fruitful discovery that a hole in a sculpture could have an aesthetic function comparable to that of a projection. Duchamp's brother, Raymond Duchamp-Villon (1876–1918), produced in his *Horse* (1914) one of the most powerful sculptural expressions of animal and mechanical energy in that period. The Belgian Georges Vantongerloo (1886–1965), accidentally exiled in Holland during the war, joined the *De Stijl* group and carved or constructed works in which the group's programmatic rectangular relationships are brought into physical space. Expressionist sculpture in Germany looked to primitive and pre-Renaissance art forms for inspiration but adhered to the human figure and rarely went far beyond some limited degree of distortion. In England at this time, the American-born sculptor, Jacob Epstein (1880–1959), modelled himself closely on African primitives.

NEW IDEAS IN ARCHITECTURE

Much of the radical work done by architects between 1900 and 1920 aimed at finding a comprehensive form embodying the constructional possibilities offered by glass, metal and concrete. Some architects, like the Frenchman, Auguste Perret (1874–1954), demonstrated the suitability of reinforced concrete for post-and-lintel buildings of a fundamentally classical character. Le Corbusier (Charles-Edouard Jeanneret 1887–1965) in his early work combined an instinctive classicism with a realistic and functional view of human needs and structural opportunities. His *Dom-Ino* project for reinforced concrete housing demonstrated a logical use of concrete and implied maximum flexibility for internal divisions and external cladding. The

55. **Ludwig Mies van der Rohe.** *Project for Glass Skyscraper.* 1920. A forerunner of the rectangular glass towers of his later years, this early work by Mies shows him exploiting the angularity, transparency and reflecting function of glass architecture with almost Expressionist warmth.

56. **Vladimir Tatlin.** *Monument to the
Third International.* 1919–20. Wood, iron
and glass. Remnants of this maquette are
stored in the Russian Museum, Leningrad.
Tatlin's project for a vast monument, new
both as architecture and as sculpture, is
an extreme example of the radicalism and
optimism that together swept through the
Russian art and design world during the
years of the Revolution.

57. **Hans Poelzig** (1869–1936). *Chemical
Factory, Luban.* 1911–12. A work of remarkable primitivism that recalls some of the
visionary designs produced in France
during the last years of the eighteenth
century.

German architect, Ludwig Mies van der Rohe (born 1886), whose career opened with a number of refined designs in a Neo-Classical idiom, made projects for glass-clad sky-scrapers in 1919–20 that combined functional severity with an almost Expressionist regard for the effects of transparency and reflection that such buildings could produce. In the same years the Russian Constructivist, Tatlin, projected a vast glass-and-iron tower that would be a *Monument to the Third International* and would at the same time contain buildings with facilities for conferences and lectures, broadcasting, administrative functions, etc., housed in a glass cylinder, a glass cone and a glass cube, all revolving at different speeds, the whole to be more than twice the height of the Eiffel Tower. Among the most impressive works to be executed in these decades were two German buildings that take little note of new materials and techniques but show the personal note already found in the adventurous work of leading designers of the later nineteenth century. Hans Poelzig (1869–1936) in his Chemical Factory at Luban (1911) created a remarkably severe and primitive building that is at once functional and expressive in the dramatic way favoured by architects of the French Revolutionary period. More expressionist in the modern sense is the *Einstein Tower* (1919–21), designed by Erich Mendelsohn (1887–1953), which looks as though it had been moulded by hand and was in fact designed to be built of poured concrete but had to be executed in bricks covered with cement. Like Tatlin's project, the Einstein Tower is both a monument and a functional building, containing laboratories and an observatory.

A combination of cool rationalism in planning with an expressive use of form was proposed by the Futurist architect, Antonio Sant'Elia (1888–1916). The *Manifesto of Futurist Architecture*, published on July 11, 1914, over his signature though not actually formulated by him, defines the problem of the modern architect: 'to raise the new-built structure on a sane plan, gleaning every benefit of science and technology, settling nobly every demand of our habits and our spirits, rejecting all that is heavy, grotesque and unsympathetic to us (tradition, style, aesthetics, proportion), establishing new forms, new lines, new reasons for existence, solely out of the special conditions of modern living, and its projection as aesthetic value in our sensibilities.' It appears that what our modern sensibilities demand is very much a style, non-historical and more akin to the forms of bridges and liners than of conventional buildings, but his projects show this style functioning within original and far-sighted conceptions of modern city planning. His clusters of buildings connected by multi-level roads suggest the fulfilment, on a vast scale, of Boccioni's dreams of modern sculpture.

58. **Erich Mendelsohn.** *Einstein Tower, Potsdam, near Berlin.* Designed 1919, completed 1921. Intended for construction in concrete (but actually executed in cement-covered brick), the Einstein Tower appears hand-formed rather than built—a sculptural monument at the same time as a utilitarian structure.

59. **Antonio Sant'Elia.** *La Città Nuova Project.* 1912–14. Ink on paper. $20\frac{3}{4} \times 20\frac{1}{2}$ in. (53 × 52 cm.). Museo Civico, Como. Architecture could have achieved dramatic modernism that Futurism dreamt of. Sant'Elia's projects, none of which was ever realised, were exhibited in 1914 and offered a realistic solution to the problem of integrating the technological world with the traditions of urban life.

1920-1940

After the heroism of 1900–1920 the art of the succeeding twenty years seems quiet and in some respects regressive. Certainly the first world war left Europe exhausted in spirit. Several artists who had shared in avant-garde activities now retired to more or less academic positions to produce art that is often hollowly traditional behind a veneer of slick modernism. Picasso's work in the early twenties, though constantly shot through with his ebullience and brilliance, is Neo-Classical at heart. Matisse continued to fashion works of high sophistication and his activity seemed to be unaffected by changes in the political and cultural climate. Similarly Bonnard, living in the south of France, untouched by the clamorous world, painted joyous visions of landscape, or interiors or figures, working mostly from memory and striking a perfect balance between an Impressionistic regard for colour and soft pictorial textures and his strong sense of pictorial organisation. The heroes of painting between 1920 and 1940 were, on the whole, the protagonists of the earlier period, now working in less lime-lit positions.

Some of the movements that had sprung up before 1920 continued to play important roles. The *De Stijl* group, for example, grew in membership and reputation through the propaganda efforts of van Doesburg, who also tried to bring the group's ideals into architecture through collaborative projects undertaken with the young architect, Cornelius van Eesteren (born 1897). Mondrian, now living in Paris, continued to work in the idiom he had created without even momentarily departing from it. In 1925, he resigned from *De Stijl* because van Doesburg wanted to change the idiom he was using from one based on vertical-horizontal relationships to one based on diagonals which he called Elementarism and for which he claimed greater dynamic force. This apparently minor change in fact struck at the roots of Mondrian's work. The vertical and horizontal co-ordinates of his art were to him the timeless principles of all man's constructive work and symbolically the most meaningful marks. They also corresponded to the urban environment and could thus collaborate with it. Van Doesburg's arbitrary rejection of the idiom revealed his superficial attachment to the principles he had been preaching. Rather than leading to greater dynamism, Elementarism resulted in a relaxed and decorative art which merely created conflict at the edges of the surfaces it occupied, thus emphasising its confinement within those edges (whether canvas or walls), whereas Mondrian's work is notorious for the commanding and ordering influence it exercises over the space in which it hangs.

60. **Theo van Doesburg.** *Aubette Restaurant-Cinema, Strasbourg.* 1926–8. In decorating one of the rooms in a reconstructed eighteenth-century house, van Doesburg applied to ceiling and walls his newly invented version of Neo-Plasticism, Elementarism. His coloured rectangles, set at 45 degrees to their surroundings, create a dynamic and ultimately chaotic ensemble. Other rooms were decorated by Arp and his wife, Sophie Täuber-Arp. The building no longer exists.

During the twenties van Doesburg was in fact making allegiances in various directions. Under his usual (adopted) name he spoke for the *De Stijl* group and also involved himself in the Suprematist and Constructivist movements that took root in Germany in the early twenties after having been displaced from Russia. One of the most active Russians to emigrate to Germany was El Lissitsky (1890–1947). Lissitsky and van Doesburg joined forces in Germany, organised exhibitions together and published joint manifestos. Under another name, I. K. Bonset, van Doesburg was active in the Dada movement, particularly in Germany and Holland. His partner in a series of lecture evenings was Kurt Schwitters (1887–1948), a fine nonsense poet and the composer of a long symphony of basic oral sounds, who made pictures out of all the flotsam and jetsam of civilisation and in his house in Hanover gradually built up an environmental assemblage of rubbish that spread through three storeys.

SURREALISM

In Paris, Dada was transformed into Surrealism. Some of the Zürich Dadaists moved to Paris around 1920, and found there a literary Surrealist movement exploring the possibilities of spontaneous writing and considering the implications of the new theories of psychoanalysis for artistic activity. Under the leadership of the poet, André Breton, a Surrealist movement embracing literature, painting and sculpture was organised. Breton defined the meaning of Surrealism in a manifesto published in 1924, and in 1925 there was the first exhibition of Surrealist art. Surrealism spread widely during the next fifteen years and was one of the forces from which the new American painting of the post-1945 period emerged. The theory of Surrealism in art is briefly as follows: that in our dreams and in those moments when our imaginations overwhelm our intellects, associations and images rise into our consciousness that are much more relevant to our real existence than the conventional subject-matter traditionally used in the arts. Some of this had been recognised before in the field of literary creation. German writers around 1800 often spoke of poetry arising from man's unconscious. Drugs were used by writers like Baudelaire and de Quincey to facilitate access to the unconscious. The Surrealists saw a particularly significant forerunner in the pseudonymous Comte de Lautréamont (1847–70) who, in a melodramatic epic entitled *Les Chants de Maldoror*, provided the apologists of Surrealism with a stock of quotations: 'as beautiful as the chance encounter of a sewing-machine with an umbrella on an operating table'. The thrill of semi-recognition that such images evoke was certainly one of the aims of Surrealist painters. Men like Max Ernst (born 1891) and Salvador Dali (born 1904) saw painting as a means of recording with hypnotic accuracy such anti-rational inventions, and they created complex pictorial metaphors of uncertain and thus unlimited meaning. Ernst also explored the use of automatic and 'found' techniques, like taking rubbings from floorboards (one is reminded of Leonardo's words about finding images in marks on old walls) and dribbling paint on to a canvas. The most important painter to emerge through Surrealism is the Spaniard, Joan Miró, (born 1893), who developed a very free and personal language of painting, often involving colour-washed canvases on to which he paints childlike images of people and things. Miró visited the United States for the first time in 1947 but was one of the most important Europeans to influence developments already under way there. In his recent work, which relates to essays he had made in the thirties, there are signs of a return influence on him from America.

PICASSO AND SOCIAL COMMENT

Picasso, as alive to events around him as to the wide world of art past and art distant, was affected by Surrealism without accepting the limitations it implied. In the later twenties his work showed stylistic elements derived from Surrealism and also, more significantly, sounded a note of stridency characteristic of the movement but not of him. Out of a fusion of Cubist and Futurist elements and Surrealist feeling, and under the impetus of political events that affected him closely, Picasso produced in 1937 one of the masterpieces of European art in *Guernica*, a large picture rather like a powerful altarpiece, commemorating the destruction of a Spanish village in 1936 and pointing to the agonies that man inflicts on man. Those who commissioned the work were disappointed that Picasso had not chosen a more realistic idiom that the man in the street would understand, but *Guernica* remains a meaningful work while more realistic attempts at political and social commentary have almost always faded as quickly as the journalism they emulate. Although many have tried, few artists have succeeded in finding a viable compromise between the aesthetic demands of modern art and their need to communicate with a wide, average public. Even the best of them, like the Belgian painter, Constant Permeke (1886–1952), managed to reach a wider public than that normally offered by the galleries. Instead, the man in the street's enthusiasm goes to the titillating charms and elaborate academic technique of Dali's 'hand-painted dream photographs'. Even in Mexico, where a group of bold and energetic painters worked with the support of the government to develop an indigenous art, real contact with the populace could not be achieved. From the 1920s on, Rivera, Orozco, Siqueiros and others presented themes of national concern in great murals where motifs derived from the Mexican Revolution and the pre-Columbian history of Mexico were mixed into an essentially European idiom.

GERMAN PAINTERS

In Germany, politically and financially bankrupt after the war, many artists felt bound to bring their work into the service of social progress. George Grosz (1893–1959) used elements from Futurism and Expressionism and particularly from the graphic work of Klee, to make sharp protests

61. **Pablo Picasso.** *Guernica*. 1937. Oil on canvas. 11 ft. 6 in. ×
25 ft. 8 in. (3.5 × 7.8 m.). On extended loan to The Museum of
Modern Art, New York, from the artist. Commissioned to
commemorate the destruction of a Spanish village by German
bombers, Picasso created a monumental and almost monochrome composition expressing terror and destruction in generalised and almost religious terms.

at the rottenness of the world around him, in much the same
way as Kurt Weill did verbally and musically in his *Three-
penny Opera*. Others remained detached from these aspects
of life, or saw their function in confronting social disorder
with ordered and harmonious art. Klee worked quietly and
unceasingly, drawings, prints, paintings and occasional
sculpture coming from his hand in quantitative and stylistic
profusion. There seemed to be no limit to his inventiveness.
Just as Schwitters used any bits of rubbish that came his
way, so Klee made his art out of any linear motifs, colours,
techniques and media that presented themselves. His work
75 in the twenties ranges from rich figurative fantasies of
patent complexity to the apparently childishly simple
chequerboards of colour. It was his habit to work on several
pictures at one time and these were often of very different
kinds. What all his work shares is a sense of preciousness,
as though Klee said to himself that any mark or material
would do but that once it was made or used it had to
be respected and justified. In a lecture he gave in 1924
he described the artist's function as the humble one of
transmitting inner and outer experiences into works of art
just as the trunk of a tree draws up the sap from its roots and
transmits it to its crown of foliage—'and the beauty of the
crown is not his own; it has merely passed through him.'

From 1921 until 1930 Klee taught at the *Bauhaus*, a design
school opened in 1919 and directed by the architect
Gropius until 1928. The school changed its character considerably, but Klee, concerned as teacher principally with
lectures investigating the elements of art and with guiding
the work of the weaving department, was affected neither
by the Bauhaus's initial Expressionism nor by its subsequent dogmatic attachment to so-called basic shapes and
colours.

Another teacher at the Bauhaus, which attracted to itself
several outstanding artists but did not concern itself for
long with the fine arts, was Kandinsky who returned to
Germany from Moscow in 1921 and joined the school staff
in the following year. In Russia Kandinsky's style had
changed from the Abstract Expressionism of the previous 74
years to a clear-cut, highly organised and sophisticated
idiom distantly related to Malevich's. For some years he
had investigated the specific qualities of particular colours
and forms, and through his new work he intended not only
to express his sensations, but also control their impact on
the beholder. These investigations provided the basis for his
theory lectures at the Bauhaus, some of which were
published in 1926 as *Point and Line to Plane* (one of a series of
books by members of the staff and by outsiders such as
Mondrian and Malevich, published by the Bauhaus). It
has become a key text in the teaching of modern art.

TOTALITARIANISM IN RUSSIA, GERMANY AND ITALY

In Russia, Lenin's economic reforms, and the change of
political climate they symbolise, led to a complete change
of attitude towards avant-garde art. After 1921, most of the
important artists of the revolutionary period left Russia,
several of them under the pretext offered by a large ex-

(Continued on page 129)

67. Piet Mondrian. *Composition with Red, Yellow and Blue.* 1930. Oil. 19 × 19 in. (48 × 48 cm.). Collection: Alfred Roth, Zürich. Between 1920 and 1940, Mondrian worked ceaselessly on a series of paintings all employing the same limited language of forms and colours which he called Neo-Plasticism, and which for him represented the whole range of visual experiences condensed into an infinitely variable formula of relationships. Extreme as his discipline may seem, it was reached logically and gradually, from the warmly realistic Dutch landscapes via his out-standingly beautiful and subtle Cubist compositions. Nihilistic as it may seem, to Mondrian it meant inclusiveness rather than a negation, universality rather than an attachment to specific experiences. Against the discords and accents of daily life he erected objects of controlled expression within which tensions and oppositions could be harmoniously contained.

68. **Kurt Schwitters.** *Hair-navel picture (Merz picture 21B).* 1920. Oil on board with painted relief of wood, cloth, earthenware and hair. $35\frac{3}{4} \times 28\frac{1}{2}$ in. $(91 \times 72.5$ cm.$)$. Lords Gallery, London. Schwitters' poetic use of urban debris gives his pictures a satirical and nihilistic note. But they are also affirmative, in that the various qualities of the ingredients he gathers are made to contribute to an essentially harmonious whole. He gave to all his works (pictures, poems, sculptures and constructions) the general title *Merz*, meaningless but suggestive. This picture is inscribed '*Merz ist nicht Dada*' — *Merz* is not Dada.

69. (left). **Max Ernst.** *The Elephant of the Celebes.* 1921. Oil on canvas. 49¼ × 42 in. (125 × 107 cm.). Collection: Roland Penrose, London. One of a group of paintings done by Ernst in Cologne during 1921–2, in which fantastic images are presented in an intentionally un-ingratiating manner. It was bought by the French poet, Paul Eluard, and in 1922 Ernst himself moved to Paris where his work provided the basis for the art side of the Surrealist movement then forming.

70. **Joan Miró.** *The Carnival of Harlequin.* 1924–5. Oil on canvas. 26 × 36½ in. (66 × 93 cm.). Albright-Knox Art Gallery, Buffalo, New York. Using the traditional theme of domestic interiors (to which he returned in 1928 under the influence of Dutch seventeenth-century painting), Miró here presents one of his most Surrealist visions, at once humorous and sinister.

71. **Joan Miró.** *Triptych.* 1937. Oil on celotex. 54¼ × 69¾ in. (138 × 177 cm.). Collection: Mme Marie Cuttoli, Paris. After a period of more Surrealist and symbolic work in the 1920s and early 30s, Miró developed a firmer and flatter manner of painting that continued through much of his subsequent work and was of wide influence. His use of the triptych familiar in late-medieval and Renaissance art is interesting (but see plate 40). It has been used quite frequently by younger artists during the last twenty years.

72. **Salvador Dali.** *The Swan of Leda.* 1959. Alexandrite and emerald. (Executed by the jeweller, Carlos Alemany of New York). Collection: Mme. Dali. Dali's jewellery, as much as his painting, exploits the disconcerting effects of ambiguous imagery. Here the inverted swan suggests the head of an elephant.

117

73. **René Magritte.** *Threatening Weather.*
1928. Oil on canvas. 21¼ × 28¾ in.
(54 × 73 cm.). Collection: Roland Penrose, London. With the dead-pan technique of a primitive, the Belgian Surrealist,
Magritte, presents conceptual clashes that
mock both the world of reason and the
world of visual communication.

74. **Wassily Kandinsky.** *Black and
Violet.* 1923. Oil on canvas. 30¾ × 39½ in.
(78 × 100 cm.). Collection: Hans and
Walter Bechtler, Zürich. In his paintings
of the 1920s, Kandinsky looked for a more
controlled means of expression than is
found in his earlier abstract work, basing
his new experiments on his own research
and that of other artists and psychologists
into the affective properties of shapes and
colours.

75. **Paul Klee.** *Senecio.* 1922. Oil on linen. 16 × 15 in. (40.5 × 38 cm.). Kunstmuseum, Basle. A particularly fine example of Klee's painting at a time when his work was especially varied and experimental. Although its free-hand geometry suggests the formal tendencies of Cubism, *Senecio* is without its spacial preoccupations, and owes more to the refined colour relationships associated with Matisse. In many respects, the art of Klee synthesises characteristics that had hitherto been assumed to be irreconcilable.

76. **Constant Permeke.** *The Betrothed
(Les Fiancés).* 1923. Oil. 59½ × 51¼ in.
(151 × 130 cm.). Musée d'Art Moderne,
Brussels. Of those painters who have tried
to involve their art directly in the social
struggles of our century, the Belgian,
Permeke, is one of the most convincing
and successful. The vigorous simplicity of
his forms, learnt from Cubism, is supported by a subdued range of colours that,
for all their expressive earthiness, are
often of remarkable subtlety.

77. **Henry Moore.** *Recumbent Figure.* 1938.
Green Hornton Stone. 54 in. (137 cm.),
high. Reproduced by Courtesy of the
Trustees of the Tate Gallery, London.
In 1948, Henry Moore was awarded the
International Sculpture prize at the
Venice Biennale in recognition of his
eminence in the world of modern sculpture. That this recognition should be
achieved by a British sculptor is remarkable enough: the history of sculpture in
Britain had been far from glorious for
several centuries. That it should be
achieved by a coal-miner's son from
Yorkshire makes it even more remarkable.
Yet in some ways this also illuminates the
event. Moore is not a fundamentally revolutionary sculptor in the way that Picasso,
Brancusi and Gabo are. His role is that of
the synthetist. He has clearly been influenced by Brancusi and Arp. He has
also learnt much from archaic Greek and
from Aztec sculpture. He took up the
theme of 'truth to materials' and turned
what could have been a functionalist
dogma into the basis of a vital relationship
between artist and matter. Most important, he brought to these influences and
ideas a strong and undisguised vein of
common human emotion, and it is perhaps his successful communication of such
emotion through sculpture which is modern without being aggressive, and which
manages to be at once classical and subjective, that gives him his wide and enthusiastic public today and assures his place
in modern art history. The timeless theme
of woman—lover, earth-goddess and
giver of life—dominates all Moore's work,
is accessible to all, and relates directly to
just those organic forms of nature which
Moore finds in the structure of his carved
materials.

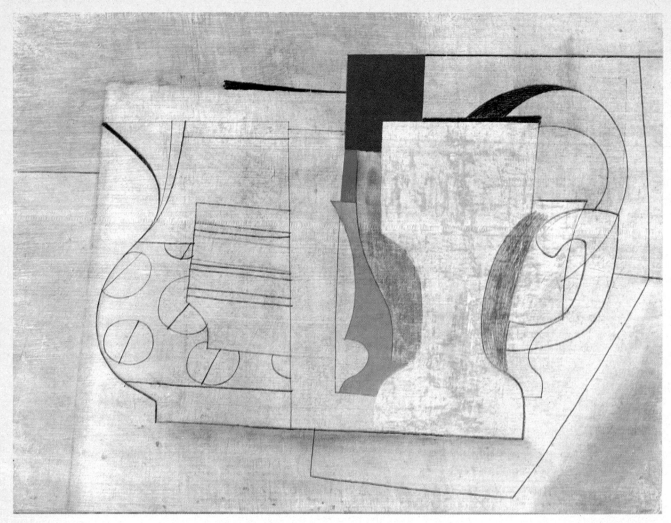

78. **Ben Nicholson.** *Lilac and Goblet:*
June 16th, 1947. Oil on board. 11¾ × 16
in. (30 × 40.5 cm.). Gallery Beyeler,
Basle. Nicholson's fine compositions of
colour areas and partly independent
linear structures belong both to the world
of abstract art, and to the long traditions
of landscape and still-life painting. He was
the first British painter to assimilate
modern developments on the Continent
and to evolve a personal (and perhaps
recognisably national) idiom from them.
He was also one of the first painters any-
where to ignore the barriers between
abstract and representational art that
had been thrown up on the Continent
between the wars.

79. (opposite, below). **Paul Nash.** *Land-*
scape from a Dream. 1938. Oil on canvas.
26½ × 40 in. (67.5 × 101.5 cm.). Reproduced by courtesy of the Trustees of the
Tate Gallery, London, and the Paul Nash
Trust. Painted a year after the large
Surrealist Exhibition in London, this picture shows how Nash (and other British
painters at this time) fused Surrealist elements of symbolism and conceptual multiplicity with an essentially Romantic vision
of landscape. Nash wrote in 1937: 'To
contemplate the personal beauty of stone
and leaf, bark and shell, and to exalt them
to be the principals of imaginary happen-
ings, became a new interest'.

80. (below). **Piet Mondrian.** *Victory*
Boogie-Woogie. 1943–4. Oil on canvas.
50 × 50 in. (127 × 127 cm.). Collection:
Mr and Mrs Burton Tremaine, Meridan,
Connecticut. In New York, where
Mondrian spent the last four years of his
life, a new excitement began to show in
his work, giving it an almost Baroque
character as against his strictly Neo-
Plasticist series (plate 67). The brashness
and pace of the city deeply affected the
elderly and solitary man who, by extending his idiom very slightly, was able
to bring a sense of rhythmical action into
his last pictures, of which this, left unfinished at his death, is the most vigorous.

1938.Z,8. Coelin- Frucht

81. **Paul Klee.** *Coelin Fruit.* 1938. Paint mixed with gum on paper. $14\frac{1}{4} \times 10\frac{3}{4}$ in. (36×27.5 cm.). Klee Foundation, Berne. A characteristic example of Klee's 'late style', that is, one of a group of works showing a roughly similar combination of strong line and harmonious (though very varied) colours, all done during the last three or four years of his life.

82. (above). **Gerrit Thomas Rietveld.** *Schroeder House,* Utrecht. 1924.
83. (right). *Red-Blue Chair,* 1917. Stedelijk Museum, Amsterdam.
Rietveld's famous chair is a remarkable early application of the Neo-Plasticist idiom to three-dimensional design. Note the use of primary colours, and also the black horizontal and vertical frame whose members do not penetrate each other but retain their integrity. In the same way the I-beams on the exterior of the Schroeder House rise against (rather than into) the balconies which they support. Here too primary colours and rectangular relationships underlie the entire design, inside and out. The physical austerity of the chair is compensated for by the lively colour.

The house, for all its apparent severity, has an air of relaxation and ease. Rietveld's Neo-Plasticist designs go far towards justifying Mondrian's dream of an environment whose refined harmony would make all 'fine art' redundant.

84. **Frank Lloyd Wright.** *Taliesin West,* near Phoenix, Arizona: the office and home of the architect. Wright's architecture fuses personal with tradition qualities in a unique way. Taliesin West suggest primitive indigenous building conventions while also embodying its designer's original conception of planning and construction.

85. (below). **Le Corbusier.** *Still-life with Many Objects.* 1923. Oil on canvas. $44\frac{3}{4} \times 57\frac{1}{2}$ in. (114.5 × 146 cm.). On loan to the Musée d'Art Moderne, Paris. (Artist's Collection). The Purist art of Le Corbusier and Ozenfant represented an attempt to cleanse Cubism of its romantic and subjective elements its ambiguities and illusionism. Here everyday objects are knitted together to form a clear and harmonious structure that can easily be understood.

86. **Jean Dubuffet.** *Metaphysic.* 1950. Oil on canvas. 44¾ × 35¼ in. (113.5 × 89.5 cm.). Collection: Mr and Mrs Arnold H. Maremont, Winnetka, Illinois. Dubuffet's exploitation of urban scrawls and thick paint is, like all successful primitivism, highly sophisticated. Special importance attaches to his reintroduction of the human image, however stereotyped (or archetypal), into a kind of painting that had concerned itself almost exclusively with effects of colour, texture and weight.

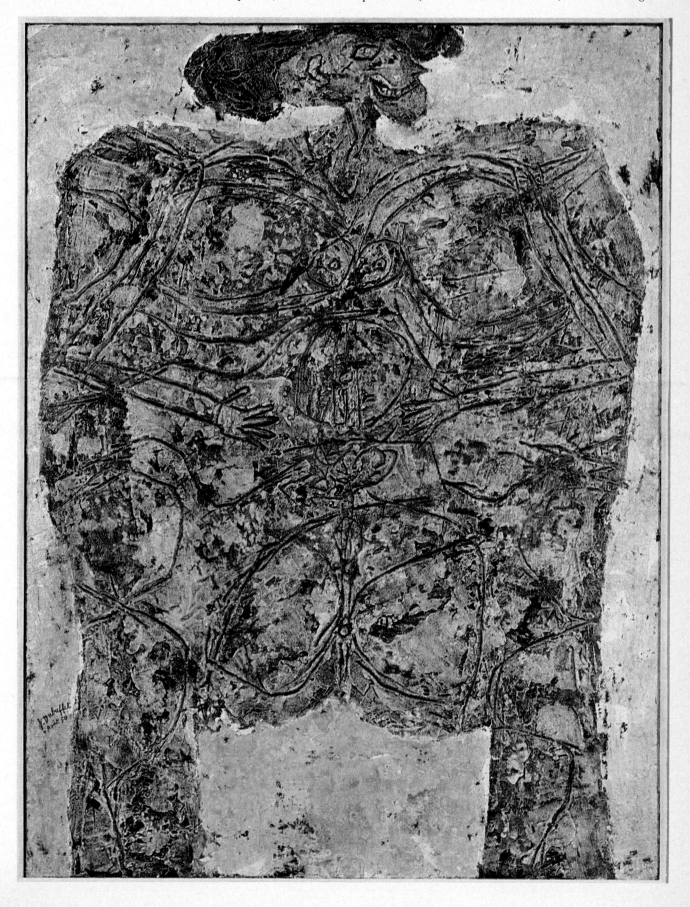

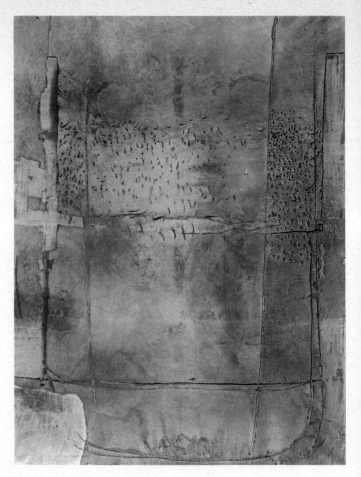

87. **Nicolas de Staël.** *The Park of Sceaux.* 1952. Oil on canvas. 63¾ × 45 in. (162 × 114 cm.). The Phillips Collection, Washington. The mature work of de Staël moves between complete abstraction and a broadly simplified kind of representation that is rooted in Synthetic Cubism. It is, however, as a handler of paint and an orchestrator of sonorous colours that he assumed a leading role in European painting since the last war, in spite of his short career.

88. **Antonio Tapies.** *Grey Ochre.* 1958. Oil, latex and sand on canvas. 102½ × 76¾ in. (260 × 195 cm.). Collection: Anthony Denney. (On loan to the Tate Gallery, London). Tapies is the best known painter involved in what has appeared to be a Renaissance of Spanish art under the influence of Paris. The lugubrious luxuriousness of his paintings is held to reveal characteristically Spanish qualities.

89. **Georges Mathieu.** *Is.* 1964. Oil on canvas. 38 × 77 in. (96.5 × 195.5 cm.). Gimpel Fils Gallery, London. In Mathieu's hands the rendering of action becomes a brief and dramatic performance in which elegance and freshness compensate for a very limited range of gestures.

hibition of Russian art to be shown in Berlin in 1922; others fitted in with the new demands of the government and are lost to view. Similarly in Germany the accession to power of the National Socialists was soon followed by their attempt to eradicate modern art. Many artists of all kinds emigrated. Those avant-garde artists who remained were forbidden to work. Works of art were removed from museums, galleries and private collections, to be sold abroad or destroyed. Adventurous directors of public galleries were dismissed. It was art's duty to glorify Hitler, the Third Reich and the Aryan race; anything else was denounced as a Jewish or Bolshevist attempt to undermine German virtue, or as the product of sick minds and charlatans. Several exhibitions of 'degenerate' art were organised, the biggest of which took place in Munich in 1937 and included work by more than a hundred artists going back as far as Liebermann.

Fascism in Italy was less concerned with culture—Mussolini himself took no interest in it—and such patronage as it exercised it gave to academic art. But even before Fascism became powerful, Italian artists themselves retired from the front-line positions taken up by the Futurists. Not only did they take a renewed interest in the art of the past (Carrà wrote a well known book on Giotto, published in 1924), but many of them renounced their own earlier radicalism.

The violence with which totalitarian governments repressed all modern art and tried to impose a fixed style and function upon it is a measure of art's important role in the spiritual life of man, and of modern art's anti-authoritarian influence. The remarkable fact must be stressed that such violently opposed ideologies as Fascism and Communism gave their support to exactly the same kind of art. There are signs at present of some loosening of governmental control over art in Russia, and some artists appear to be moving away from Social Realism, but it is clear that after more than forty years of enforced sterility it must be a long time before Russia can again contribute to the development of modern art.

DEVELOPMENTS IN BRITAIN

Far from destroying modern art, totalitarian measures helped to propagate it in other places. Great Britain and America benefitted particularly from emigrating artists. In Great Britain, the influx of foreigners coincided with the emergence of the first English painter of international **78** significance since Turner. Ben Nicholson, (born 1894), knew Paris and Cubism, and in the early thirties began to use the conventions of Synthetic Cubism as the basis for elegantly constructed and delicately painted still lifes. In 1934 and 1935, he visited Mondrian and was deeply impressed by the tranquillity of his art and personality. Between 1934 and 1939, Nicholson carved a series of white-painted reliefs that, without in any way imitating Mondrian's work, have something of his intuitive approach to order. From 1938 to 1940, Mondrian lived in London, an

encouraging presence for the pioneers of abstraction in England. The thirties saw also the emergence of Henry Moore and Barbara Hepworth as outstanding sculptors, and the tentative re-entry of Britain into the field of modern architecture. The most powerful movement in British art in the thirties, however, was Surrealism. A British Surrealist group organised an international exhibition of Surrealism in 1936, and *The London Bulletin* was published as a Surrealist magazine of art and literature. Herbert Read emerged as a champion of Surrealism and of modern art generally. The appeal of Surrealism in Britain is to be explained partly in terms of the strong literary element that easily dominated its aesthetic content, and partly in terms of the movement as an essentially Romantic mode of vision to which the countrymen of William Blake could easily respond. Before 1936, some painters, like Paul Nash (1889– **79** 1946), had already brought aspects of Romantic British landscape painting into metaphorical expression that was close in spirit to Surrealism. After 1939, when the war isolated Britain and dispersed her avant-garde groups, several painters (outstanding among them Graham Sutherland) worked independently in styles that moved between Romanticism and Surrealism.

THE 1930S

On the whole, the 1930s were a dark decade for modern art. With large areas of Europe closed to living art by totalitarianism, and with the often academic works of Surrealism exerting a powerful appeal over a confused world, it must have seemed that the aesthetically more creative forms of modern art had lost the day. With the closing down of Moscow, Paris became more than ever the centre of modern art, with Munich, Berlin, Milan and Rome as competitors. The more literary forms of painting and superficially modernised forms of academicism dominated the scene. Mondrian worked in Paris from 1918 until 1938, but few people took any interest in his work and he did not have a single exhibition during those twenty years. The more worldly-wise Kandinsky, who worked in Paris from 1933 until his death in 1944, made rather more impact, and an international group met there to discuss abstract art, but they found little interest or encouragement and it is remarkable how few of its members were French.

Klee left Germany in 1933 and spent the remaining years of his life in Switzerland. From 1935, he became increasingly ill, but his work flourished. His productivity if anything increased, his paintings tended to become larger, and for the first time much of his work coheres stylistically. In many of the paintings of 1935–40, heavy painted lines act with **81** and against colour patches, making a new alliance between his powers as draughtsman and as colourist. But at the same time he continued to explore quite different kinds of pictorial imagery and the last year of his life, one of the most productive of his career, saw him attempting new things that at times seem to foretell the post-war adventures of much younger artists.

62. **Antoine Pevsner.** *Developable Surface.* 1936. Brass rods. 26½ × 12 in. (67 × 30 cm.). Philippe Dotremont Collection, Brussels. Pevsner's constructions, elaborate developments of a simple theme, appear to be the nuclei of energies that penetrate the surrounding space.

SCULPTURE IN THE 1920S AND 1930S

In the sculpture of these decades the most creative work was, as we found with painting, the achievement of a surprisingly small number of individuals, often working in seclusion. No great movements comparable to Cubism, Futurism and Constructivism arose to confront sculptors with new plastic concepts. Constructivism, condemned in Russia, flowered in the hands of the brothers Gabo and Pevsner. Gabo left Russia in 1921. The next twelve years he divided between Paris and Berlin, he then came to England in 1933 and went on to the United States in 1946. Pevsner settled in Paris in 1923 after two years in Berlin, and worked there until his death in 1962. In the work of both, Constructivism becomes detached from the aesthetic of Cubism and finds its own logic. Both started from mass-less reliefs and figures using thin sheets of material resembling the painted planes of Analytical Cubism and exhibiting something of that style's compositional simplicity. Pevsner, who had been a painter, moved from this into a remarkably austere style and method that owed much to his interest in mathematics. Using straight linear elements 62 (wire or rod), he constructed works of sculpture that still have the compositional directness and thus monumentality of Cubism. At the same time, through the curvature and interpenetration of the planes formed by his lines and through the implications of physical movement in and beyond the works themselves, his sculpture possesses exceptional energy and richness. Gabo's work has tended to be more obviously personal and meditative; paradoxically, it was he who had studied engineering. In the first years of the 1920s, he made a series of models for monuments and buildings that may represent an attempt to justify experimental art to the pragmatically inclined Russian authorities but may also be seen as counterparts to the glass skyscraper projects of Mies van der Rohe and as contrasts to Mendelsohn's Einstein Tower. Subsequently he moved away from such projects to self-sufficient works in a variety of materials, trying to realise complex relationships with forms that are themselves surprisingly simple and using materials that offered the maximum of insubstantiality. The development of plastics came to his aid, and it is in a long series of constructions based on this versatile material that his career finds its climax. Here sculpture, without ceasing to be apprehensible as a physical object, achieves an extraordinary fluency and lyricism—light and space are brought into expressive play.

Among the growing number of artists of many nationalities who attached themselves to Constructivism, Moholy-Nagy and Calder were particularly inventive and influential. Laszlo Moholy-Nagy (1895–1946), who was born in Hungary, developed a form of Constructivism that embodied his personal vision of a technologically transformed world of clear forms and shining surfaces. He was as 64 interested in film and photography, in typography and industrial design, as in pure art, and during 1923–8 he helped to transform the Bauhaus into the industrially

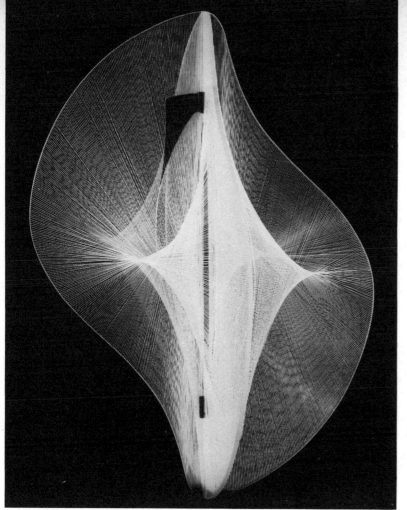

63. **Naum Gabo.** *Linear Construction, No. 2.* 1949. Perspex and nylon thread. 36 in. (91 cm.). Stedelijk Museum, Amsterdam. Gabo's exploitation of plastic materials brought into Constructivism a quality of lyricism that cannot have been envisaged when the movement first expounded its principles but which is in no way contradictory to them.

64. **Laszlo Moholy-Nagy.** *Light-Space Modulator.* 1922–30. Movable construction, steel, wood and plastic. $59\frac{1}{2} \times 27 \times 27$ in. ($151 \times 68.5 \times 68.5$ cm.). Busch-Reisinger Museum, Harvard University. Space and movement has been one of the most persistent themes in modern art. In his mobile constructions Moholy-Nagy gave physical reality to the space, movement and light implied in his paintings and photograms.

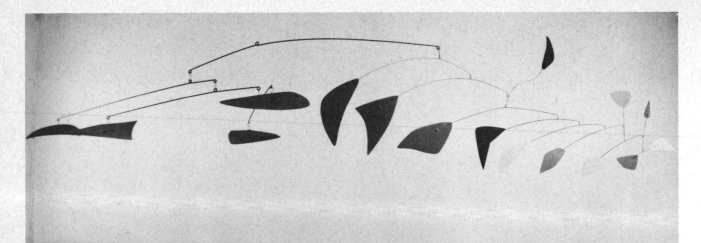

65. **Alexander Calder.** *Red Toenail,
Blue L.* 1962. Metal construction.
36 × 150 in. (91.5 × 381 cm.). Grosvenor
Gallery, London. The mobiles of Calder
are poetic and often gay interpretations of
natural movement in terms of abstract
forms and colours.

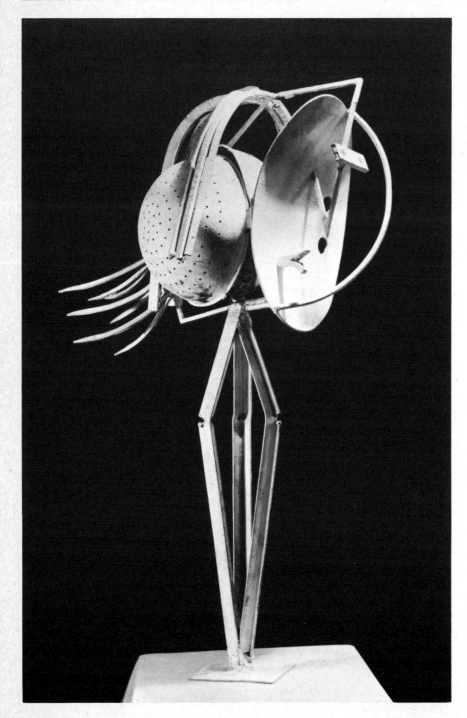

66. **Pablo Picasso.** *Head.* 1931. Wrought
iron. 39½ in. high (100 cm.). Collection:
the Artist. The freely expressionistic constructed sculptures of Picasso are the
progenitors of countless welded-metal
sculptures produced all over the world,
and themselves are indebted to African
constructed masks.

centred institution that became famous. His coolly romantic constructions of shining metals, often with moving parts
to be seen under dramatic lighting, are the fullest expression
of his enthusiastic spirit. From 1935 until 1937, Moholy-
Nagy worked in London. Then he settled in Chicago and
started there the *New Bauhaus* and so developed and propagated ideas that he had also set out in two deeply influential
books, *The New Vision*, published by the Bauhaus in 1929
(an English edition appeared in 1947), and *Vision in Motion*,
published in Chicago in 1947.

If light is the common denominator of Moholy-Nagy's
pursuits, movement is the principal concern of the American, Alexander Calder (born 1898). Calder's parents were
artists, but his own early interests lay in tools and in engineering. Working in Europe, he made himself a reputation
for wire sculptures, then invented a series of motorised and
hand-propelled sculptures with moving parts, and in 1931
65 began to produce mobiles in which finely balanced members are set in motion by air currents or by the touch of a
hand. Their formal ingredients are abstract but they often
hint in their general forms at trees, waterplants, and so on.
Although technically they are constructions, they do not
share the aesthetic qualities normally sought by Constructivism and suggest a spiritual kinship with Surrealism
rather than any other movement.

PICASSO, ARP, BRANCUSI

A different kind of constructed sculpture, markedly expressionist in character, was initiated by Picasso in 1930
when he began to fashion three-dimensional objects out of
66 odd pieces of scrap metal. As a creative process this was
more akin to the rubbish pictures of Schwitters and to
Picasso's own wood and cardboard reliefs of 1913–4 than to
Constructivism with its accent on clear and abstract forms
and modern materials. But the scrap yards, too, are part of
the modern world, and Picasso's inventive handling of this
material has been one of the most fruitful contributions to
modern sculpture. At about the same time he produced a
series of 'stick statuettes', usually between fifteen and
twenty inches in height, which he carved from long strips
and sticks of wood and then had cast in bronze. Here expressionist distortion meets the Constructivist ideal of a
massless sculpture inserted into space, as Picasso looks
back to the primitive forms of archaic Mediterranean
sculpture.

Arp's work developed considerably during the 1920s and
30s. He gave less time to two-dimensional and relief work
than during the Dada years, and was encouraged by Surrealism to exploit ambiguities of form and meaning in
sculpture that took on a more and more biomorphic
character. Using various materials interchangeably, Arp
modelled forms that suggested a great variety of objects
and experiences while always asserting life and physical
well-being. Like Klee, he believed in the essential natural-
ness of art—'art is a fruit that grows in man, like a fruit on
a plant, or a child in its mother's womb'—and his personal

67, 68. **Jean Arp.** *Birds in an Aquarium. c.* 1920. Painted wood
relief. $9\frac{7}{8}$ × 8 in. (25 × 20.5 cm.). Collection, The Museum of
Modern Art, New York. (Purchase). *Human Concretion.* 1949
(original 1935). Cast stone (original, plaster). $19\frac{1}{2}$ in. high
(49.5 cm.). Collection, The Museum of Modern Art, New York.
(Gift of the Advisory Committee). Arp's optimistic sense of life
and of the human warmth of rounded and nestling forms,
penetrates his entire production. The poetic yet precise idiom
he developed offered an invaluable counterpart to the impersonal and geometrical abstraction that emerged in
Holland and Central Europe in the 1920s.

inclinations allowed him to develop his art into forms buoyant with life.

Undoubtedly the greatest sculptor at work during these decades was Brancusi, who continued to carve his tough and primitive-looking wood sculpture, and to model and carve his deceptively simple refined forms. At times he would produce a carved marble sculpture and also a modelled and cast version, in which case he would adapt the original form in various scarcely noticeable ways to make it more suited to its new character. Often he used highly polished bronze for the cast version, himself polishing the metal with almost obsessive persistence. As a result, the form of the original, often rounded and expressive of mass and weight, seems to become immaterial as its surface reflects everything around it. During this time Brancusi's reputation spread widely, especially to the United States where he had the first of a series of important exhibitions in 1926. It was on that occasion that the American Customs refused to allow the normal duty-free entry for works of art to his *Bird in Space*. There followed a lawsuit to establish that what the officials took to be a piece of machine metal of industrial origin and function could be, and in this instance, was, a work of art. Eminent witnesses were called on both sides, and ultimately judgement was given in Brancusi's favour.

BRITISH SCULPTURE

It was partly under the influence of Brancusi that Britain, until then a land without sculpture of more than local interest, entered the international arena. With the emergence of Henry Moore (born 1898), England could boast a sculptor abreast of the Continental avant-garde and at the same time profoundly original. Moore can be seen as a synthesiser of various trends. From Brancusi he learnt the value of allowing the material to command the character of the work; Surrealism and Arp revealed to him the multiplicity of meanings found in familiar forms; certain technical devices he developed from the examples of Archipenko and Gabo. Michelangelo was a root influence on him, as well as archaic Greek sculpture and the carvings of pre-Columbian Mexico. Moore himself brought an instinctive response to the physical world and to its qualities of scale, texture and mass, and echoed them in sculptures that were often variations on the timeless theme of the reclining female figure. In these he fused into miraculous unity suggestions received from the human image, from landscape forms and from the structure of the material itself. Brancusi once said: 'Your hand thinks and follows the thoughts of the material', and Moore has spoken similarly about the creative process as a kind of dialogue between the artist and the wood or stone under his hand. Barbara Hepworth (born 1903) also appeared in the thirties as an important new sculptor. While her work has been more totally abstract than Moore's, it is more immediately human and intimate than his. He tends towards the dramatic and the monumental; she creates forms that respond

69. **Oskar Schlemmer** (1888–1943). *Abstract Figure, Sculpture in the Round.* 1921. Nickelled bronze. 48⅛ in. high (107 cm.). Marlborough Fine Arts Gallery, London. In his paintings, sculpture and ballets, Schlemmer tried to fuse the ancient tradition of idealised human form with his time's consciousness of mechanistic materials and shapes.

to deeply personal needs. She remains the only woman artist to have brought specifically feminine sensations to her work and to have realised them in terms that have universal meaning.

ARCHITECTURE IN THE 1920S AND 1930S

In architecture the twenties and thirties mark a climax and a triumph. As patronage began to lose its fears of modernism, new architecture began to arise in many countries and in some quantity, and it presented a remarkable unity of appearance. The precepts and projects of *De Stijl* and Suprematism, and the stylistic inclinations of two or three outstanding architects—notably Le Corbusier, Walter Gropius and Mies van der Rohe—fused to form what has become known as the International Style.

The one full embodiment of *De Stijl* principles in architecture is the Schroeder House in Utrecht (1923–24), designed by Gerrit Rietveld (1888–1964). Preserving the

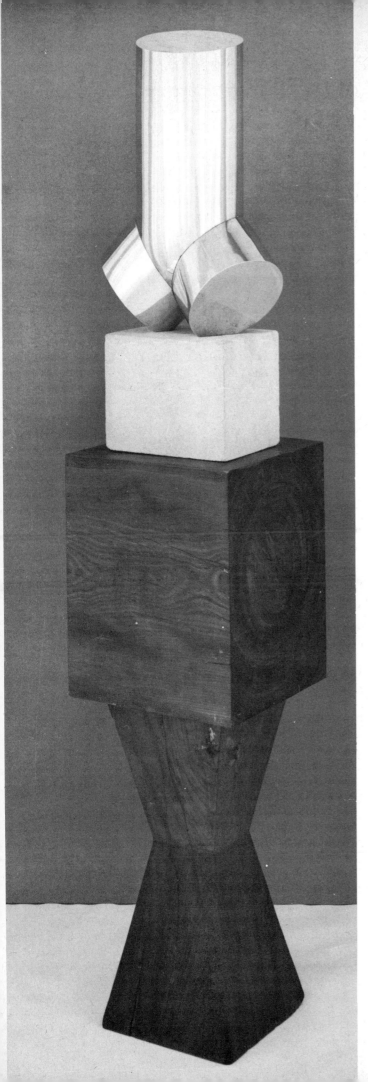

70 (left). **Constantin Brancusi.** *Torso of a Young Man.* 1925.
Polished bronze on limestone, wood base. 60 in. high (152.5
cm.). Collection, Joseph Hirshhorn, New York. At first sight a
sculpture of mechanistic severity, this torso soon reveals an
extraordinary sensuousness of form and surface that is then
stressed and complemented by the character of Brancusi's substructure.

71 (above). **Constantin Brancusi.** *King of Kings—The Spirit
of Buddha.* 1937. Wood. 118¼ in. high (300 cm.). The Solomon
R. Guggenheim Museum, New York. In this carving, for which
Brancusi selected an old and weathered piece of oak, the Rou-
manian peasant in him comes to the fore; for once a modern and
sophisticated artist actually joins hands, as an equal, with the
makers of primitive tribal artifacts.

72. **J. J. P. Oud.** *Workmen's Houses, Hook of Holland.* 1926–7. After adhering to the Neo-Plasticist idiom of the *De Stijl* movement, Oud here introduced into his masterpiece a few curved elements, making for a greater fluency of form. These terraces are the first outstanding example of low-cost housing of high quality design.

73. **Le Corbusier.** *'Plan Voisin' town-planning project, Paris.* 1922–30. Le Corbusier conceived the high-rise building as a vertical street or neighbourhood, situated in a beautiful and healthy park environment and well separated from traffic arteries.

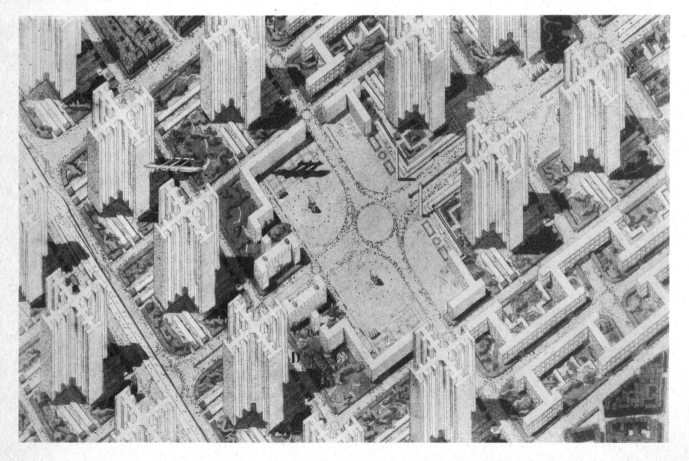

identity of each plane and stanchion, Rietveld juxtaposed the elements of his building with great delicacy and emphasised their independence by the use of contrasting colours. Another architect associated for a time with the *De Stijl* movement was J. J. P. Oud (born 1890), the designer of a colony of workmen's houses in the Hook of Holland (1926). In one of his essays published by the Bauhaus in the same year Oud spoke of 'the need for number and measure, for cleanliness and order, for standardisation and repetition, for perfection and high finish; the properties of the organs of modern living, such as technique, transport and hygiene in the sphere of social conditions, mass-production methods among economic circumstances'. These words express some of the concerns shared by the leading architects of this period, and they show that although functionalism (that is, exclusive attention to material considerations as the source of architectural form) was often used to justify their designs, they were conscious also of aesthetic needs. This is as clear from Rietveld's hovering playing-card rectangles as from the almost endless horizontals and unbroken concrete surfaces of Oud's housing.

LE CORBUSIER

It is above all clear from the work of Le Corbusier, the great propagandist of functionalism ('the house is a machine for living in'), who, in his first book *Towards a New Architecture* (1923), pointed enthusiastically to the design and serial manufacture of aeroplanes, liners and cars as model expressions of the modern age, and to Greek temples as comparable instances of unfettered modernism in their time. His rationalism and his classicism are at bottom inseparable, which is another way of saying that Le Corbusier is an outstanding example of the tradition of French classical architecture, going back to the sixteenth century. During the 1920s, Le Corbusier began to be recognised as the leading young architect in Europe, partly through his writing and polemical projects and partly through the relatively few buildings he was allowed to realise. The projects included plans for the rebuilding of part of Paris with enormous skyscrapers set into parkland the first demonstration of a new kind of urban planning that has since been put into practice on a much more modest scale in many places. In 1927, he won first prize in a competition for the League of Nations Palace to be built in Geneva and, although his design was not used for the Palace, it has been an important prototype for the planning of building complexes of this type. The private houses he built at Garches (1927) and at Poissy (1929–31) combine the basic ideas he had expressed in his *Dom-Ino* diagram of 1914 with his belief in traditional systems of proportion and in the basic geometric solids which, like Plato, he considered of their essence the most beautiful forms. Thus, in his search for a new order he returned to principles and values which we saw being discarded at the beginning of this book.

74. **Le Corbusier.** *Villa Savoie, Poissy-sur-Seine.* 1929–31. An instinctive classicist, Le Corbusier gave a clear and carefully proportioned external form to his villa, while shaping its interior with a freedom that rested on his separation of the carrying function of columns from the dividing function of walls.

75. **Ludwig Mies van der Rohe.**
Dining-room. Tugendhat House, Brno, Czechoslovakia. 1930. Mies's refined economy of form is matched by his attachment to perfectly beautiful and, at times, luxurious surfaces. Compare this interior with Le Corbusier's *Dom-Ino* diagram, figure 54.

76. **Walter Gropius.** *Bauhaus Building, Dessau, seen from the air.* 1925–8. The most famous building of the 1920s, Gropius's Bauhaus synthesises avant-garde architectural ideas from all over Europe. The decoration and furnishing of the interior was undertaken by the Bauhaus workshops.

77. **J. A. Brinkmann, L. C. van der Vlugt** and **Mart Stam.** *Van Nelle Tobacco Factory, Rotterdam.* 1927–30. One of the most go-ahead buildings of the 1920s, this factory remains an outstanding example of functional design even while it embodies some of the stylistic predilections of its time.

ARCHITECTURE IN GERMANY

In Germany, Mies van der Rohe showed himself to be an exceptionally sophisticated and thoughtful exponent of the International Style, particularly in the German Pavilion he designed for the international exhibition in Barcelona *75* (1929) and the Tugendhat House in Brno, Czechoslovakia (1930). He ennobled the style by his use of fine materials (chromium-plated steel columns, marbel, onyx, ebony) and by the unique delicacy of his detailing; austerity and clarity of form was accompanied by the organic lavishness of selected surfaces. Historically the most important monu- *76* ment of the period was, however, the new Bauhaus Building in Dessau (1925–6), designed by Walter Gropius (born 1883): an informal composition of rectangular units with clean white concrete surfaces and large unbroken areas of glass covering the workshop block. The lettering on the outside of the building and the furnishings inside were de- signed by the staff and students of the school, so that the whole offered a magnificent demonstration of modern de- sign. In 1929, Gropius was given an opportunity, in the Siemensstadt flats commissioned by an electrical company for its employees, to involve himself more deeply in the social issues which, he has always insisted, are the founda- tions of architectural design. The long 'slab' blocks he erected there have continued to be the most frequently used alternative to the 'point' blocks proposed on a vast scale by Le Corbusier.

'MACHINE AESTHETIC' AND THE
INTERNATIONAL STYLE

Thus the development of geometrical abstraction, so bril- liantly initiated in Holland and Russia, became the aesthe- tic basis of the international avant-garde in architecture at a time when it faltered in painting. While Mondrian's work was almost ignored and Malevich had to abandon his

78. **I. A. Golossef.** *Zoueff Club, Moscow.* 1927. An example of the bold architecture produced in Russia during the 1920s.

pioneer position, architects paid homage to the new language they had demonstrated. But on the whole this tribute was unconscious. The clear forms and logical appearance of *De Stijl* and Suprematist art fitted the twenties' vision of the new technological world so closely that designers forgot that it was essentially a style they were handling, a set of conventions and not an ineluctable law. The general term 'machine aesthetic', invented by van Doesburg in 1921, was used for this set of conventions although they owed little to the forms and functions of machines. Adherence to these conventions tended to become a moral issue among modernists. At the Bauhaus, for example, where they were taught as the basis of all design, students were accused of aesthetic treason if they departed from them, although, as is obvious to us, there is no real reason why chairs and lamps and chess-sets should be designed on the basis of right-angles, spheres, primary colours, and so on. The International Style, for all its virtues as a harmonious and unifying idiom, gave the designer the dangerous illusion of working in close alliance with modern technology when in fact it isolated him from the realities of technology almost as completely as the Neo-Classical designer of around 1800 was isolated from the industrial revolution of his time.

The United States, too, came under the spell of the so-called machine aesthetic, especially once Bauhaus teachers and ex-students began to arrive there. But the United States also had two major opponents of it. Frank Lloyd Wright had spoken of 'the Machine Age' as early as 1901 but he saw the machine as something that had to be dominated by individual genius. Gropius preached teamwork; Wright the duty of subjective expression. And although some of his earlier work had heralded the International Style, after 1920 it was often marked by violently idiosyncratic mannerism and the adoption of exotic influences such as that of pre-Columbian Mexican temple architecture. One of the most powerful monuments to Wright's originality and megalomania is Taliesin West in Arizona, began in 1938. This complex of buildings, school, design office, living quarters all in one, is made of great bulwarks of 'desert concrete' (concrete poured round locally found rocks) and a light superstructure of angled timber beams and canvas. It has been suggested that, consciously or unconsciously, Wright had conceived these buildings to make an impressive ruin for a future age, and we recall Soane's romantic vision of his own building as a victim of time. The other opponent of the International Style, and for quite different reasons than Wright's, was Buckminster Fuller (born 1895), who would seem to have been the only man of that period to have faced the realities of functional design. He saw that new techniques and new social conditions invited a radical reconsideration of the bases of design. His Dymaxion House project of 1927 consisted of a hexagonal ring of plastic dwelling units hanging round an aluminium core of services. It is a project that still stands totally apart from the world of architecture as we know it and it remains one of a very small number of attempts to link mass-produced housing to the opportunities offered by technology and not to the old habits of building industries. Fuller's geodesic domes, which can be built in any size and of almost any material—aluminium, plastic, cardboard for example—have been used in a very limited way. Fuller's example is a standing reproach to the men who shape our houses and towns and to those who commission them.

88

84

80

79. **Robert Maillart** (1872–1940).
Schwandbach Bridge, near Schwarz-Canton, Berne. 1933. Curved concrete slabs. Through technical expertise and inventiveness, an engineer like the Swiss, Maillart, is able to find new forms of construction that at times influence architectural design.

80. **Buckminster Fuller.** *Geodesic Dome for the Union Tank Car
Company maintenance and repair facility at Baton Rouge, Louisiana.*
October, 1958. Steel and plastic. 384 ft. span, 128 ft. high
(117 × 39 m.). Architects have as yet taken little notice of the
potentialities offered by new materials and new techniques, of
which Fuller's multi-purpose domes are relatively simple
examples. They come in all sizes and materials: this one, in
spite of its size (its volume is 23 times that of the dome of St
Peter's in Rome), is very light and cheap to erect.

Since 1940

During the last twenty-odd years the arts, particularly painting, have regained the momentum they lost after the first world war. Again movements spring up in rapid succession and manifestos are thick upon the ground.

Varieties of art, abstract and figurative, vie with each other as the most suitable modes of expression for our time, while national differences tend to diminish as vast exhibitions congregate the world's art product in one place and richly illustrated magazines spread knowledge of the latest developments into libraries, studios, galleries and homes on every continent. The traditional divisions between the arts, already smudged by earlier generations, are ignored more and more. Pictures become three-dimensional, are liable to produce sounds, and at times aim at the environmental completeness previously limited to architecture. Sculpture moves, makes sounds, projects luminous images, and has even been known to perform its own immolation. Architecture extends into regional planning. No one can say with any certainty which artist and which work will take their place beside the old masters, though each of us has his favourite candidates, but we need have no doubt that while much of the vast quantity of art and architecture that is produced each year is of little enduring value, it includes work of great beauty and significance. Although there are dangers in the great scale of art activity to which we are accustomed, one of its effects has been a partial closing of the gap that had arisen between the artist and the average man. There are signs that, before long, art may become a matter of popular interest.

Since the last war, New York has assumed artistic leadership and has become the great centre for important exhibitions. Also there has been a remarkably wide acceptance of abstract art. The abstract work between the wars had not, as we have seen, met with much interest. In recent years, non-figuration has become the dominant idiom in western art and enlightened forms of figurative art have tended to be undervalued. It is probably true to say that while our awareness of the wide range of possibilities within abstraction has grown, and we have learned (what once seemed impossible) to distinguish good abstract art from bad, our sensitivity to many aspects of representational art has diminished. Nevertheless, we are justified in thinking that so far the greatest achievements in recent painting have been in the field of non-figuration.

ABSTRACT EXPRESSIONISM IN EUROPE

The years immediately following the war saw what amounts to a rediscovery of Abstract Expressionism. In so far as abstraction had lived on in the twenties and thirties it had been dominated by the intuitive but carefully controlled 'classical' abstraction of men like Mondrian and Kandinsky. Now it was a freely spontaneous kind of abstraction that once again became important. The earlier work of Kandinsky had contributed to this, but aspects of the art of Klee and Miró have a deeper kinship with it.

In France, artists like Bazaine and Manessier built up large colour harmonies on patterns that were found instinctively but became habitual. Nicolas de Staël (1914– **87** 55), an outstanding colourist and handler of paint, used landscape and other motifs as the framework for sonorous colour compositions of great beauty. Germany and Italy, emerging from their years of barbarism, produced many painters similar to these, working with or without references to the visible world, but concerned with finding a relationship of form and colour that could be taken to correspond with the personality of the artist. An extension of this pursuit was what came to be called 'matter painting', which often involved building up thick layers of paint (or paint mixed with a filler such as plaster) on the picture and then working in this pastose surface as though it was a large wax tablet. Jean Dubuffet (born 1901) used this technique most **86** effectively for unnaturalistically figurative ends, schooling himself on the scrawls with which the modern urban primitive expresses his loves and hates on walls and doors. In Spain, particularly, matter painting evoked a rich response, as though the country of Velasquez and Zurbaran and of glowing austerity recognised itself in this art. Inspired by the example of Paris, a sufficiently large number of Spanish painters appeared rather suddenly and attracted attention on the international scene to warrant talk of a renaissance in Spanish art. Antonio Tapies (born 1923) has been the **88** most successful of these, handling his pastes with all the elegance of a Parisian yet achieving a peculiarly Spanish note in his gloomy surfaces. The Italian, Burri, once a doctor, has been making pictures out of sackcloth and paint, sheets of steel and, most recently, sheets of plastic, translating, it would seem, the horrors of war into fashionable wall decorations. All this art, one feels, bears a burden of gentility and sweetness that few Europeans are able to escape. Though individual artists such as de Staël and Dubuffet have contributed more lastingly, the one through the relative strength of his colour compositions, the other through the new and richly emotive kind of figuration, informal abstraction on the Continent has seemed self-indulgent and unregenerative compared with contemporary work produced in the United States.

THE UNITED STATES

America had, of course, been aware of developments in modern European art. American collectors had been among the first to support Matisse, Picasso and others. In 1913, the large Armory Show introduced New York to a wide range of avant-garde art. American artists travelled continuously across the Atlantic to inform themselves at first hand of what was happening in Paris. During the thirties the United States was more isolated culturally as she coped with her recession. Then around 1940, a considerable number of important European artists arrived in New York. Mondrian, Ernst, Masson, Léger and others **58** worked in America for a few years, Mondrian even achieving a remarkable vigorous variation of his abstract **80** idiom under the influence of the life and rhythm of the big city. It is possible to point to particular instances where the influence of these Europeans has made its mark on American painting, but their most important effect was that of nudging American art out of the regionalism that had overtaken it. The outcome was an art that rejected Europe, or attempted to reject Europe, rather than develop from European premises. The new American painting that burst upon the world between 1948 and 1950 prided itself on ignoring the traditions, particularly of Paris, and on finding its roots principally in the present condition of man and his environment; if it did owe something inevitably to the example of living and dead European artists, it also looked westwards to the Orient, especially to the calligraphic art of Japan and to the philosophy on which this art was founded. A forerunner in this respect was Mark Tobey (born 1890) who in the 1930s, together with the English potter, Bernard Leach, travelled in China and Japan and studied in a Zen monastery in Kyoto. In the thirties and forties he developed a calligraphic style of

91 painting, his 'white writing', in which he spins cosmic webs of frequently quite small dimensions. In their all-over optical texture, avoidance of compositional accents and suggestion of pictorial depth, they are objects for peaceful contemplation. But contemplation and the search for peace implied in it are not characteristic of recent American painting.

POLLOCK AND DE KOONING

92 The hero of the new painting was Jackson Pollock (1912–56). In 1947 he began to produce his drip paintings, dribbling strands of paint on to a canvas stretched out on the floor and worked on from all sides. He, too, was spinning a web, but to do it he brought his whole body into activity, working on impulse and with irrational desire rather than to a plan or a specific image. The following statement, written in 1947, pin-points his relationships with his picture and has been as influential as the pictures themselves: 'When I am *in* my painting, I'm not aware of what I'm doing. It is only after a sort of "get acquainted" period that I see what I have been about. I have no fears about making changes, destroying the image, etc., because the painting has a life of its own. I try to let it come through. It is only when I lose contact with the painting that the result is a mess. Otherwise there is pure harmony, an easy give and take, and the painting comes out well.' His paintings are often very large. Physical involvement demands an area large enough to permit freedom of action, and small enough to be spanned by the traces of paint. These, swinging across the canvas, create sensations of space and movement of a kind heralded by Klee and by Tobey but which are new to painting on this scale and with this energy. Klee had always insisted that a picture manifests the process it embodies as much as an image or a subject, and now here was a kind of painting in which the process itself was the subject. The American critic, Harold Rosenberg, named it Action

Painting. In spite of some European and American critics who tended to mock it as empty display, Action Painting during the fifties found many followers in Europe, though their performances on the whole justified the critics' contempt. Pollock's own work has retained its energy and beauty.

At the same moment another kind of Action Painting, more clearly charged with violence and passion, was dem-

94 onstrated by another American, Willem de Kooning (born 1904). Working with a large, well-loaded brush, and using aggressive gestures that seem destructive but contribute to the gradual formation of an image, de Kooning builds threatening and sometimes benevolent firmaments of colour. At times these incorporate particular subjects, as in his *Woman* series with its presentation of the female as the feared and desired object, inescapable to men as the sea is to the lemming. De Kooning's form of Abstract Expressionism, descended from the more violent aspects of European Expressionism, has had a wide influence and on the whole a more beneficial effect than Pollock's. But their bipartite demonstration that painting is essentially the art of making a compelling mark on a surface, and that one variable way of making this mark compelling is to produce it out of inner compulsion via explosive physical action, has had a profound and liberating effect on painting all over the western and the westernised world. It issued a ringing challenge to the Paris-centred tradition of 'fine' painting, though of course it demanded alternative skills of its own, and drew attention to the extent to which respected European painting had become dominated by technical elegance and taste. Set against the new American painting, Kandinsky's Abstract Expressionism, while based on a similar programme, also appears inhibited by taste, and, more important, is read more as a picture of an emotional condition than as the condition itself. Kandinsky's paintings are representations; Pollock's and de Kooning's are presentations.

OTHER AMERICAN PAINTERS

The example of Pollock and de Kooning affected not only younger artists. Painters contemporary with and older than themselves were able to discard conventional inhibitions and move out into similar fields of untrammelled activity. Some of them worked towards a greater simplicity. 'The progression of a painter's work, as it travels in time from point to point, will be toward clarity: toward the elimination of all obstacles between the painter and the idea, and between the idea and the observer. ... To achieve this clarity is, inevitably, to be understood.' These words were written in 1949 by Mark Rothko (born 1903), at the 96 moment when he was perfecting the profoundly original mode of painting that has made him famous: fine veils of colour that seem to be hung over each other in symmetrical, monumental arrangements, ceaselessly affecting each other's appearance and particularly their spatial positions, creating sensations of majesty and mystery of a kind scarcely known since the decline of Byzantine art. Pollock's lines of paint, often exhibiting between them the bare canvas and thus emphasising their super-imposition upon it, had finalised the process initiated in Synthetic Cubism: of the picture as existing not in an illusionistic space behind the surface on which it is painted but on or in front of that surface. With Rothko's painting, largely through the interaction of his softly brushed in areas of colour, the surface of the picture identifies itself with the margin of colour that surrounds all the others, and since that colour is activated by the others, the surface itself appears to become part of the general instability, an apparently continuous shifting of the colours in space that seems to belong neither behind nor in front of the canvas. This lack of containment in depth (Rothko's pictures extend forwards and backwards but are contained laterally by their edges, while Mondrian's extend laterally but are held in one plane) drew attention to the ambiguous spatial action of colour, subsequently investigated and exploited by a great number of artists. It was partly under this influence that the tradition of geometrical abstraction was revived. In Joseph Albers (born 1888) the United States has a painter who studied and taught at the Bauhaus and since 1933 on has been teaching in America and developing the tradition of classical abstraction. In his work, and generally in what was subsequently labelled 'Hard-Edge' painting, there is an element of which painters like Malevich and Mondrian had not been aware or had preferred not to exploit. This is the reaction of the retina to shapes and colours, or the effects of movement, flickering colours and after-images, that are carelessly called optical illusions. As Goethe said: 'Optical illusion is optical truth'. The conscious exploitation of such effects, together with the deliberate use of colour relationships that make for spatial flux (as in Rothko) has greatly enriched the emotive power of simply composed paintings and brought back into painting a magic quality that the puritanical leanings of several of the pioneers of modern painting and also the physical bravura of much Abstract Expressionism had tended to exclude. It also demands a relaxed and unhurrying attitude from the spectator: the modulations of image and mood that such paintings offer only reveal themselves in time and to a patient observer. And from the painter they demand an approach that is the reverse of Action Painting. Clarity of design and colour is normally a pre-requisite for Hard-Edge painting, and thus a skilled and painstaking application of paint, together with great refinement in the choice of colours and composition, has been brought back into avant-garde painting. Albers, particularly, has simplified his designs and used his colours with ever-growing subtlety.

RECENT PAINTING IN BRITAIN

Great Britain, inevitably the country most open to American influence, responded swiftly to what was happening there. But even before the new American painting became known in Britain, a few artists there had broken away from the romantic naturalism that dominated the British art scene during the war. Abstract art in Britain was given a new start through the activity of Victor Pasmore (born 1908), who had become known as a painter of landscapes, interiors and figure subjects of exceptional delicacy, and suddenly rejected all aspects of naturalism in favour of abstract relationships of form and colour in two and three dimensions. His work and his teaching has profoundly influenced the course of modern art in Britain. The work of the St Ives school, a loosely related group of painters who settled in the Cornish port where Ben Nicholson worked, was certainly modified by American influence as the delicate colours and textures and formal rhythms learnt from Nicholson became intuitive gestures and often assertive forms and colours, and the atmospheric tone and space effects suggested by the climate of Cornwall were replaced by firmly interrelated colours and structures. A more vehement kind of Abstract Expressionism, embodying Surrealist elements, is represented in Britain by Alan Davie (born 1920), perhaps the only painter in the world to persevere with an entirely subjective and explosive mode of painting without any loss of vigour and incisiveness. In Belgium, Holland and Denmark, the Cobra Group (dominated by Karel Appel and Asgar Jorn) has extended the innate Expressionism of most north-European art by adopting qualities of physical aggressiveness from Abstract Expressionism for paintings that hover between figuration and abstraction. Commercial success, mostly in Paris, appears to have weakened the group's work by letting an action that must be compulsive become habitual.

RECENT FIGURATIVE PAINTING

It is undeniable figurative painting has fared less well during the post-war years, and recent attempts in Europe and America to produce or present a revival in this field have not been fruitful. It is not for lack of ability, as those nostalgic for the art of the past are wont to assume. Certainly figuration demands its particular skills, and it has already been suggested that we may have become less responsive to them, but there is in fact no lack of serious and solid painting of the human figure—only a lack of figure painting that transcends the act of recording to reach the level of creative art. For the figurative artist of today has to prove the relevance of representational painting, just as Mondrian and his contemporaries had to justify their exclusion of the visible world. The boldest and finest figurative painters of our day are elderly. Picasso continues to this day to exercise his hard-won freedom to paint anything and in any manner he pleases. Among his recent productions are pictures that resemble his own Analytical Cubist work, others that seem to be heavy-handedly patterned pictures in an Art Nouveau manner, yet others dominated by areas or flat colour akin to Matisse's (these became particularly noticeable in the years immediately following Matisse's death in 1954), and a long series of

(Continued on page 161)

90. **Stuart Davis.** *Lucky Strike.* 1921. Oil on canvas. 33¼ × 18 in. (85 × 45.5 cm.). Collection, The Museum of Modern Art, New York. (Gift of The American Tobacco Company, Inc.). Stuart Davis (1894–1964) was one of the few Americans to prepare the ground for the recent revolutionary developments in American art between the wars. This picture of a packet of tobacco, an *objet trouvé* in the manner of Duchamp but monumentalised in the process of painting, is a forerunner of Pop Art.

91. **Mark Tobey.** *Written Over the Plains.* 1950. Oil and tempera. 30 × 39¾ in. (76 × 101 cm.). Museum of Art, San Francisco. (Gift of Mr and Mrs Ferdinand Smith). Already in 1935, Tobey was exploring the constructive and expressive potentialities of the calligraphic line he had studied in China. From 1944 onwards he produced a long series of pictures in which this element was used to build mysterious images of space and time-lessness—objects for, and products of, contemplation and spiritual penetration.

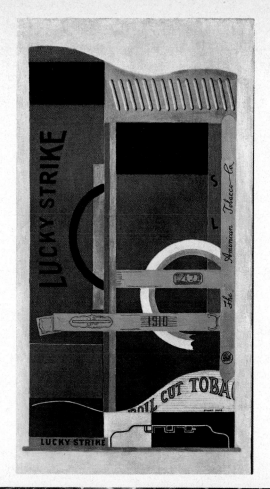

93. (opposite, below). **Arshile Gorky.**
The Limit. 1947. Oil on paper. 50¼ × 62¾
in. (127.5 × 159.5 cm.). Collection:
Mrs A. M. Phillips, London. Gorky's
abstract and very personal Surrealism
was of particular importance to the first
wave of American post-war painters and
continues to stand out as an expressive
idiom of unusual lyrical poignancy.

92. (opposite, above). **Jackson Pollock.**
Number I, 1948. Oil on canvas. 68 × 104
in. (172.5 × 264 cm.). Collection, The
Museum of Modern Art, New York.
(Purchase).

94. (above). **Willem de Kooning.**
Saturday Night. 1955–6. Oil on canvas.
69 × 79 in. (175 × 200.5 cm.). Collection: Washington University, St Louis.
The two leaders of the Abstract Expressionist movement in the United States between them demonstrated a wide range
of its possibilities. Pollock's fine web of
lines, dribbled on to a canvas and loosely
directed by his swinging arm, is principally graphic in effect: we are more conscious of lines than of paint. Differences in

colour make for a shimmering richness,
but the colours function principally as
tone and determine the apparent location
of the lines in space. De Kooning's canvases confront us as objects constructed of
paint. The big brush, heavy with colour,
is made both to build up this form and to
give it expressive character. Physical action engenders the processes of both these
painters, but Pollock's is rhythmic and
psychologically distant while de Kooning's
is at once more combative and more corrective in that his brushstrokes appear to
be in conflict with each other even as they
collaborate to form an image. This image
is sometimes figurative: de Kooning has
painted a series of female figures using
much the same technique. Pollock, too, at
times brought figuration into his pictures;
when he did so the graphic character of
his work came out even more strongly.

95. **Franz Kline.** *White Forms.* 1955. Oil
on canvas. 74 × 50 in. (188 × 127 cm.).
Collection: Philip Johnson Collection,
New York. Franz Kline (1910–1962)
emerged in New York in 1950 as one of
the leading Abstract Expressionists.
During the last years of his life he brought
colour into his work but he made his
reputation with his powerful and archetypal paintings in black on white canvas.
The title of this picture stresses the importance he attached to the 'negative'
areas left by his giant brushstrokes.

96. **Mark Rothko.** *Mauve and Orange.*
1961. Oil on canvas. 69¼ × 63 in. (176 ×
160 cm.). Marlborough Fine Arts, London. After the eruption of American Abstract Expressionism in the later 1940s,
Rothko's emergence on the international
scene was a surprise. It had not been difficult to equate the size and violence (or at
least energy) of Action Painting with the
scale and the displayed virility of America.
Rothko's unrhetorical art revealed another side: the meditative and mystical,
already indicated in a very different manner in the art of Mark Tobey, but generally more easily recognised in the work of

certain American writers. To the apparent
brashness of Pollock's and de Kooning's
techniques, Rothko opposed a precarious
delicacy of brushwork and a hyper-sub-
tlety of colour that, in its way too, was a
criticism of Parisian *cordon-bleu* painting
and at the same time rebuked Action
Painting for its conspicuous turmoil. From
this kind of painting stems a large body of
American and British painting that makes
a virtue of technical efficiency and compositional directness.

97. (opposite, above). **Sam Francis.**
Round the Blues. 1957 (reworked later).
Oil on canvas. 108 × 192 in. (274.5 ×
487.5 cm.). Reproduced by courtesy of
the Trustees of the Tate Gallery. Born in
1923, Sam Francis is one of the youngest
of the Action Painters, as well as the most
lyrical. His translucent petals of colour
float on the white canvas, recalling the
water-lilies in Monet's *Nymphéas* series.

98. (opposite, below). **Serge Poliakoff.**
Abstract Composition. 1959. Oil on panel.
1959. Oil on panel. 38 × 51½ in. (96 ×
131 cm.). Hanover Gallery, London.
Poliakoff produced his first abstract
paintings around 1937, under the influence of Kandinsky and Delaunay who
taught him to work towards the unity of
form and colour. He has said: 'If you
let it, your colour will take charge of you.
Similarly with your forms: the spontaneous form for an artist to use is always an
organic one, but you've got to be in
control of it.'

99. (above). **Josef Albers.** *Study for
Homage to the Square : See,* 1961.
100. (right). *Study for Homage to the Square:
Look,* 1962. Both oils. Both 24 in. (61 cm.),
square. Collection: the Artist. Albers' long
series of paintings based on one design and
sharing the title 'Homage to the Square'
is a particularly convincing example of
the spirit of research in modern painting.
In this series, more exclusively than in his
earlier work, he is concerned with the
power and qualities of colour. By invent-
ing for himself a repeatable design he can
concentrate his and our attention on
colour, and the particular design he has
chosen, with its spatial overtones suggestive alternatively of recession or projection, involve him in controlling the spatial
implications of his colour relationships.
Thus a painting that at first sight seems
no more than a handsome colour chord
may reveal itself as a colour progression in
space. Albers' exploitation of colour is the
climax of a creative involvement in colour
that can be compared to the Renaissance
artists' involvement in draughtsmanship.
Its earlier heroes are the Post-Impressionists (particularly Seurat, Cézanne and
van Gogh), Delaunay, Matisse and Klee.

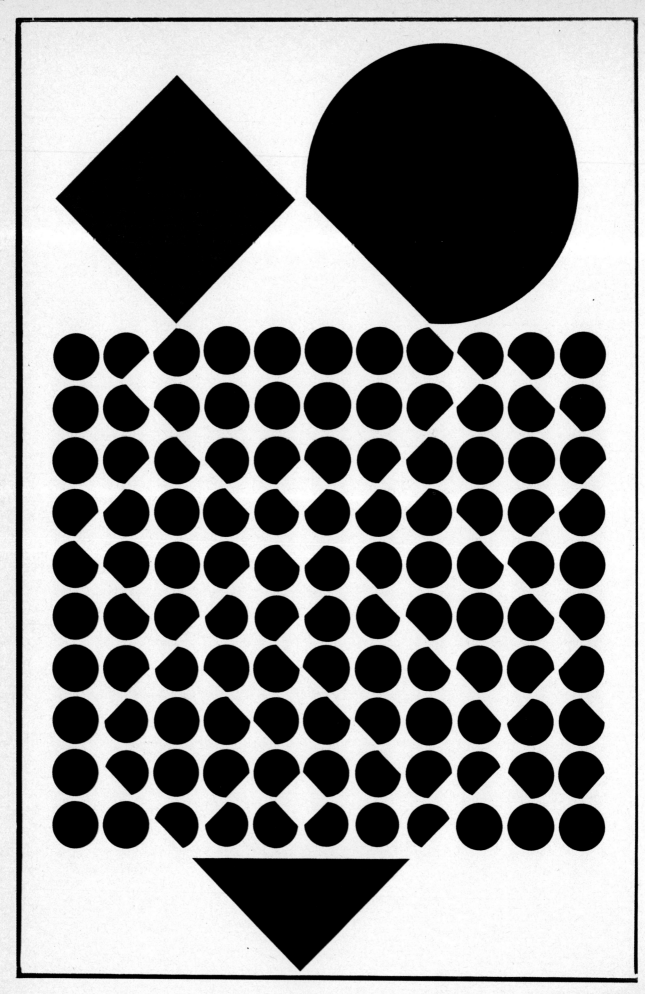

101. **Victor Vasarely.** *Cassiopée.* 1957. Oil on canvas. 76¾ × 51 in. (195 × 129.5 cm.). Collection: Denise René, Paris. Vasarely, a Hungarian who settled in France in 1930, is the father of what is becoming known as 'optical art'. With great skill and what seems to be unlimited inventiveness, he exploits in his compositions the physical effects of colour and contrast on the retina and the mental process of interpretation through which we order the information collected by our senses. This painting shows how our minds construct ambiguities out of assembled forms that are in themselves quite clear. If it is to have any artistic value, work of this kind must be more than an elaborate teasing of our perceptual habits. Vasarely's paintings are remarkable for their dignity and monumentality, and also for their refined use of colour.

102. **Henri Matisse.** *The Snail (L'Escargot).* 1953. Gouache on cut and pasted paper. 112¾ × 113 in. (287 × 288 cm.). Reproduced by courtesy of the Trustees of the Tate Gallery, London. During his last years Matisse produced a number of large and small works composed of pieces of coloured paper in which he anticipated many of the qualities of what subsequently became known as Hard-Edge painting. This is one of the large works in this series, in which the roughly spiral arrangement of the hand-coloured pieces of paper suggested the title. Others lack even this distant reference to actual objects.

103. **Victor Pasmore.** *Transparent Poly-chromatic Construction in White, Black and Indian Red.* 1962–3. Painted wood and plastic. 32 × 35 × 18 in. (81 × 89 × 46 cm.). Collection: the Artist. One of the leading figures in Britain's effective entry into the world of modern art since the second world war, Pasmore has always insisted on the inevitability of three-dimensional constructive art as a logical outcome of the demonstrations of Mondrian and other classical abstractionists between the wars.

104. **Roger Hilton.** *The Aral Sea.* 1958. Oil on canvas. 84 × 96 in. (213.5 × 244 cm.). Collection: Leslie Waddington, London. Hilton and a number of other British painters have used the free technique and imagery of Abstract Expressionism to evoke sensations of land and seascape in paintings that thus belong to both the abstract and the representational fields of art.

105. **Alan Davie.** *The Farmer's Wife. No. 2.*
1957. Oil on canvas. 7 ft. × 5 ft. 8 in.
(2.13 × 1.73 m.). Collection: Gimpel Fils,
London. The Scotsman, Alan Davie, was
one of the first painters in Britain to accept
the challenge of Abstract Expressionism,
renewed through the example of the new
American painters during the years
immediately after the second world war.
Working spontaneously, often with bright
colours and on large canvases, he sets
down and elaborates images that subsequently reveal symbolical content.

106. **Lucio Fontana.** *Gold of Venice.* 1961. Oil on canvas. 59 × 59 in. (150 × 150 cm.). McRoberts and Tunnard Gallery, London. In Fontana's work the theme of violence, so frequently found in modern art, takes on a peculiarly subtle and aristocratic form. His theoretical writings, notably his *White Manifesto 1946 (Spazialismo)*, calls for an art of space and light, with actual or implied movement. In a painting such as this the two concerns meet. The fine, luxurious field of gold, furrowed to suggest centripetal movement, is slashed with a gesture that remains active long after the event. Because the surface of the canvas has been opened, the back of the picture and the space behind it become part of the painting's world, as well as the space immediately in front of it, which the knife penetrated and the curling edges of the cut embrace. Other paintings by Fontana involve more violent gashes through a smoothly painted surface, or canvases both perforated and bejewelled. He has also produced a large range of sculpture. Fontana's writing and work has inspired a considerable number of European artists to make new ventures into harnessing space and light for art, but none has had the Italian's inventiveness, economy and acute elegance.

107. (above). **Jaspar Johns.** *White Flag.*
1955–8. Oil and collage on canvas.
$52\frac{1}{4} \times 78\frac{3}{4}$ in. (132.5 × 190 cm.).
Collection: the Artist.

108. (right). **Robert Rauschenberg.**
Odalisk. 1955–8. Wooden structure with
magazine cuttings and other materials.
81 × 25 × 25 in. (206 × 63.5 × 63.5
cm.). Leo Castelli Gallery, New York.
After 1955 it became clear that an American reaction against abstract art was
gaining momentum. Painters like Johns
and Rauschenberg, impatient with Abstract Expressionism, turned to familiar
subjects. In many instances they adopted
the free use of non-art materials sanctioned
by Synthetic Cubism to create works in
which questions of meaning are liable to
dominate over purely aesthetic content.
Because of this, and the satire that often
seems to govern their choice of motifs and
means, work of this kind has been linked
with the Dada movement of the first
world war period. But 'Neo-Dada' would
seem to be a contradiction in terms. Also
these artists are not averse to producing
art (Rauschenberg, for example, has produced an entirely serious and very moving
series of illustrations to Dante's *Inferno*);
their attack is directed more at the solemn
introspection of Expressionism than
against art as such. The Pop movement
stems largely from Johns and Rauschenberg.

158

109. **Kenneth Noland.** *New Light.* 1963.
Plastic paint. 68 × 68 in. (173 × 173 cm.).
Ulster Museum, Belfast.

110. **Anthony Caro.** *The Month of May.*
1963. Painted aluminium and steel.
9′2″ high. (2.8 m.). Kasmin Limited, London. Modern sculpture has often owed its
dominant concepts to avant-garde painting, but recently there have been signs of
a more fundamental rapprochement between the two arts. Here are two artists
handling colour-forms: the American
painter using an arrangement of heraldic
simplicity, while the British sculptor places
his forms into space with the apparent
freedom of a painter wielding a brush.

111, 112. **Le Corbusier.** *Notre Dame du Haut*, Ronchamp. (above) exterior detail, (right) interior. 1955. A turning point in Le Corbusier's development as architect, this building has also had a wide and decisive influence on world architecture by proposing an essentially personal and *ad hoc* mode of design as an alternative to the International Style. Every part of the church was designed by the architect to create an affecting environment. The interior is most poetically illuminated by small stained-glass windows set into the massive concrete wall; the altars of the two small chapels are lit from above by means of the towers.

81. **Alberto Giacometti.** *The Square.*
1948–9. Bronze. $24\frac{3}{4} \times 17\frac{1}{4} \times 8\frac{1}{4}$ in.
($63 \times 44 \times 21$ cm.). Öffentliche Kunst-
sammlung, Basle (Emanuel Hoffman
Collection). Though he does not adopt
the techniques and aesthetics of Constructivism, Giacometti too works with
space: space as a spiritual burden and as
the arena of human events.

81

spirited variations upon and (in the comedian's sense) impressions of masterpieces by Velasquez, Delacroix, Courbet, and others.

Alberto Giacometti (born 1901), principally a sculptor,
draws and paints figures trapped in a linear network suggestive of space and environment psychologically respond-
ing closely to his modelled bronze figures that appear to
shrink from the touch of light. The Irish painter, Francis
Bacon (born 1910), is acclaimed internationally for his
figure subjects based on photographs, stills from films and
reproductions of paintings. He is one of the most skilful
manipulators of paint working today, but his need to
present his painted figures, both as to situation and in the
manner of painting, as victims of aggression is made to
seem spurious by the artificiality of his models.

113. **James Gowan** and **James Stirling.**
Engineering Building, Leicester University.
1962–3. Between the wars 'functionalism'
meant little more than the justifying of
current stylistic preferences. Today, when
style as such tends to be regarded as an
unnecessary veneer, some architects have
learnt to give character to a building by
dramatising its functions. For obvious
reasons this can be done most successfully
with industrial and cultural buildings:
power-stations, factories, laboratories,
schools, libraries, concert halls and theatres. In this example, analysis of the
many requirements of the programme,
which called for lecture theatres, laboratories, offices and a large workshop area,
and of the site conditions which appear to
have suggested the repeated use of the
45° angle in the plan, presented the architects with certain formal means. These
they welcomed and from them they
fashioned the individual character of the
building. Nevertheless, styleless though it
appears to be, the building owes much to
earlier works conceived in the same spirit,
as, for example, in nineteenth-century
marine and civil engineering and the
industrial buildings designed by Frank
Lloyd Wright.

82. **Germaine Richier.** *Tauromachy.*
1953. Gilded bronze. 45 in. high (114.5
cm.). Collection, Jean Richier. During
and since the last war, a great deal of
Expressionist sculpture has wished to
warn us of death and destruction, but in
no one's work is this achieved so forcibly
and with such lasting aesthetic power as
in the modelled sculptures of Germaine
Richier.

83. **Fritz Wotruba** (born 1907). *Head.*
1954. Bronze. 16¾ in. high (42.5 cm.).
Collection, The Museum of Modern Art,
New York. (Blanchette Rockefeller Fund).
The Austrian sculptor, Wotruba, gives
monumental form to the human image by
emphasising the stereometric quality of
its forms.

In theory, the great figurative art of tomorrow should
come out of a synthesis of figuration and abstraction. This
has often been said and long been looked for. It is not being
achieved, perhaps, because it was achieved already decades
ago—most convincingly in the art of Matisse. His attachment to beautiful aspects of the visible world was equalled
and balanced by his search for total pictorial harmony,
with the result that an absolute unity was found for these
disparate elements. Cézanne had aimed at the same thing,
and in his landscape paintings he had achieved it, but his
figure subjects, perhaps because of his greater emotional
involvement in the subject-matter, have not the finality of
Matisse's.

POP ART

Meanwhile a different way back to the facts of the visible
world has recently been offered by the practitioners of Pop
Art, otherwise known as the New Realists and also by
other names. It is dangerous to generalise about the considerable range of artists (mostly American and British)
included in this category, varying as they do as much in the
quality as in the character of their work. They share a more
or less direct use of motifs from our environment in their
work, and it is their almost invariable selection of motifs
from the mass media that justifies the epithet 'Pop'. It is

satisfying to see the mass media, themselves owing so much to many phases of modern art, contributing to art in return —and now that designers are adopting Pop Art conventions and mannerisms for advertisements, and film and television titles, it seems that the style and time gap between art and commercial art has been closed at least temporarily—but one would guess that, as Pop Art seems on the whole to leave aside the basic questions and values of art it will be a short-lived movement. Indeed, it may already be over, though it will take some time for the wave of imitations and adaptions to spend itself. On the whole, there has been a general return to an exploitation of the facts of painting, with painters exploring ever further the potentialities of colour areas in loose and strict compositions, the optical qualities (and their emotional content) of interlocked forms in colour or in black and white, and other such factors arising directly from depositing pigment on a surface.

SCULPTURE SINCE THE WAR

The realm of sculpture has expanded rapidly during the last twenty years. One hesitates to point to any of the younger sculptors as the equal of men like Brancusi and Picasso (who continues to produce three-dimensional work of many kinds) in profundity and inventiveness. Giacometti, whose sculpture has been mentioned already, is certainly one of the most convincing modellers working today, fashioning his surprisingly individual and personal human images again and again without ever giving the impression of being trapped in his own idiom. In Italy, immediately after the war, there was something of a sculptural revival that leant heavily on Etruscan and other archaic prototypes and thus reminds one of the Neo-Classical wave that swept through painting in France after 1918. Marino Marini (born 1901) was the most skilful and creative sculptor involved in this development, which on the whole had little vigour of its own and has almost disappeared from the international scene. In France two outstanding sculptors emerged after the war, Richier and César. Germaine Richier (1904–59) managed persuasively what many attempted: to create human images whose distorted and decayed condition implies the brutalisation and decomposition that would follow a catastrophe of the kind with which opposed sections of the human race are currently threatening each other, and to do this without sentimentality or sensationalism. César (born 1921) initiated the use of crushed car bodies as self-sufficient sculptures—descendants of Duchamp's 'ready-mades', but particularly rich in associations and aesthetic attractions. He also uses the structural freedom and textural range of welded metal sculpture to form semi-human images of a more or less Surrealist kind. In this company the work of Max Bill (Swiss, born 1908; architect, painter, industrial designer and sculptor) stands out for its rare coolness and permanence. Of considerable variety, his sculpture always has the beauty of an abstract (often mathematical) idea

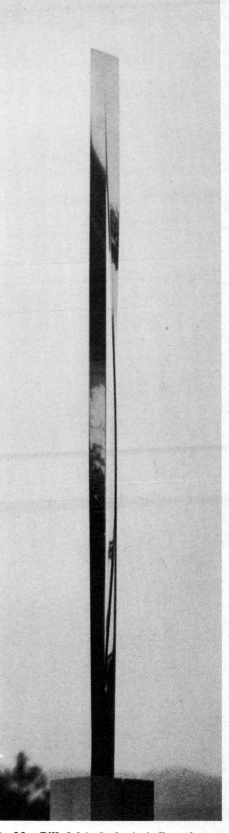

84. **Max Bill.** *Infinite Surface in the Form of a Column.* 1953–5. Polished brass. 79 in. high (200 cm.). Collection, the Artist. To the Expressionism of almost all Central European sculpture Max Bill opposes what is the ultimate in sophistication and simplicity.

realised in three-dimensional form with the utmost refinement.

Britain, at first carried along by the international postwar success of Henry Moore and Barbara Hepworth, reinforced its assault on the international world of sculpture with such men as Armitage, Butler and Chadwick. Their work ranged from direct figuration to the semi-abstract, and owed little to Moore and Hepworth. Another age-group of sculptors soon came forward: Paolozzi, Dalwood and Caro (all born 1924) brought their disparate talents to quite different kinds of sculpture. Caro's rejection of sculptural imagery and techniques in favour of a kind of lyrical Constructivism that opposes its fanciful forms and colours to the normal solemnity of international Constructivism and has the effortless quality of a few coloured brushstrokes hanging in space, has given a particular impetus to the growth of new sculpture in Britain. He claims to have been more significantly influenced by American painting than by anyone's sculpture, and it may generally be said that this influence, proving that pictures quite devoid of anthropomorphic references can confront us with sensations of human energy and presence, may yet liberate modern sculpture from its conventional, often disguised, attachment to the human form and to human scale. New materials, such as plastics, and the unconventional use of older materials enable sculptors to join with painters in creating new art objects and art situations involving the spectator in an emotive relationship rather than presenting him with a finite and self-sufficient image.

110

ARCHITECTURE SINCE THE WAR

Modern architectural design has become fully respectable since the war. Cathedrals, governmental buildings, indeed whole cities, can now be designed in a twentieth-century idiom—even if not always by the best of living architects. Technically advance seems slow, which is all the more regrettable since all over the world there is an extreme need for many new buildings. Aircraft industries and other spearhead organisations are continually researching into new materials, but architecture is tied to time-honoured practices which builders are reluctant to abandon. There have been some unusually magnificent opportunities for planning and for building since the war. The new capitals of Brazil and India, at Brasilia and Chandigarh, the rebuilding of cities destroyed in the war, like Hiroshima and Berlin, rising standards of living and the growing assets and public-relations consciousness of big business—these create a situation in which architecture can thrive, and such socio-economic problems as over-population, over-motorisation and over-urbanisation force the planner to become the medicine-man of modern society.

Stylistically, the major events have been the bringing of a very refined version of the International Style to the United States, its dissemination from there, and the relatively localised rebellions against this style by individuals and movements.

85 (left). **David Smith.** *History of Leroy Borton.* 1956. Steel. $88\frac{1}{4} \times 26\frac{3}{4} \times 24\frac{1}{2}$ in. ($224 \times 68 \times 62$ cm.). Collection, The Museum of Modern Art, New York. (Mrs Simon Guggenheim Fund). Although recent American sculpture has not shown the originality and the *élan* of American painting, some remarkable sculptors have emerged. Smith is perhaps the most remarkable of them. His welded metal assemblages adopt something of the Action Painter's freedom to make marks in space, but, as descendants of the welded sculptures of Picasso and Gonzalez they are more obviously part of the European tradition.

86. **Ludwig Mies van der Rohe.** *Seagram Building, New York.* 1957. A collaborative production by Mies and his famous disciple, Philip Johnson. At once the most splendid and the most austere of New York's business palaces.

87. **Ludwig Mies van der Rohe.** *Farnsworth House, Chicago.* Designed 1946, built 1950. A small lake-side villa, this white steel-framed house is perhaps the finest expression of Mies's sophisticated and timeless idiom.

88. **Frank Lloyd Wright.** *Solomon R. Guggenheim Museum, New York.* Designed 1943–6, built 1956–9. The great American architect's most violent gesture against the impersonal and classical character of the International Style. Inside the building a spiral ramp forms one long and continuous gallery around a vast central space.

89 (left). **Kenzo Tange** (born 1913) and **Y. Tsuboi.** *Town Hall, Kurashiki, Japan.* 1960. Since the last war, Japan has become one of the most impressive contributors to modern architecture, fusing western influences (particularly that of Le Corbusier) with her own remarkable traditions.

90 (right). **Alvar Aalto** (born 1898). *Säynatsälo: Civic Centre, Finland.* 1949–53. In his contributions to the rebuilding of Finland after the war, Aalto emphasised the native roots of his architecture which at times gave a decidedly primitive quality to his work.

The first event is associated principally with Mies van der Rohe, who settled in the United States in 1937 and brought to the commissions that have subsequently been given him a feeling for order and dignity that has not been equalled in any architecture since the Parthenon. Each problem is worked on until out of the complex of requirements and conditions there emerges a solution which has a crystalline clarity of idea and form. The utmost refinement of detailing goes with building shapes so unrhetorical and self-sufficient as to make them stand out as timeless monuments in their restless environments. If Mies imposes order on the environment, on the inhabitants of his buildings he imposes moral and aesthetic courage, for some people want to live and work in caves, while Mies offers them marvellously proportioned glass boxes that make demands on their self-confidence and brings great spiritual rewards. His influence in the United States has been profound. One of the most **86, 87** powerful architectural firms, Skidmore, Owings & Merrill, has propagated his style in many large buildings, and ver-

sions of it have been accepted all over the western world and in Japan as urbane, technically efficient and adaptable. Like, say, the Georgian style in eighteenth-century Britain, the Miesian style offers to designers everywhere an idiom that can be used at the highest levels of sophistication and can also guide much duller minds towards a decent result.

But many architects demand a more potent and more individual form of expression, and during the last ten to fifteen years there has been a marked revival in what one is tempted to describe as modern Baroque design. The pioneer here, surprisingly, was Le Corbusier whose work had been so fully imbued with the classical feeling for geometrical form. His pilgrimage church at Ronchamp **111, 112** (9150–3) looks as though it had been moulded in the hand, and he did in fact begin designing it by making small models. At the same time, we are told, it embodies his system of interrelated dimensions, published in 1950 as *The Modulor*. Until his recent death, Le Corbusier was in

91. **Louis Kahn** (born 1901). *Richards Medical Research Laboratory, University of Pennsylvania.* 1958–60. In this, his most famous building so far, Kahn has managed to embrace aspects of Frank Lloyd Wright's theory and of the International Style while giving it a picturesque silhouette reminiscent of much Romantic architecture.

complete charge at Chandigarh of the design and detailed lay-out of the city's capitol: Parliament Building, Secretariat, Governor's Palace, Law Courts and smaller ancillary buildings. In them and in their placing he combined an underlying classical concept with freely formed subsidiary elements, and the result promises to be the Acropolis of the twentieth century.

Free design is a dangerous tool in the hands of any but the most critical designers. Immediately the designs for Ronchamp were published, feeble imitations of it began to appear. But it was also a signal for more self-reliant architects to come forward. Structurally ambitious designs, departing radically from the vertical-horizontal coordinates that seem to represent the anthropomorphism of architecture, have appeared on all continents, even if they have not always been justified by the requirements they were supposed to meet. Nevertheless, in a world that must

become more and more mass-produced, in architecture as in other matters, we must welcome buildings that stand out to celebrate selected aspects and functions of life; and it follows that the rest must stand back (not in quality but in assertiveness) since there is a limit to the quantity of architectural 'gesturing' any environment can bear. Some architects have found a basis for individual expression in heightened functionalism, that is, in finding the practical solution for a given set of needs and then dramatically asserting the particular character of this solution in its forms and materials. Several of the finest and most exciting buildings of the last few years have been of this kind, and it may well be that we have here a fruitful synthesis of classical and unclassical elements in a union that is particular to each building yet remains closely related to human activities, and, since it does not depend on stylistic conventions, is infinitely renewable.

Epilogue

During the 170 years we have surveyed, the character of art and of artists has changed dramatically. Our story began with a sweeping revolution, visible and latent, and this revolution would seem to have prompted an accelerating chain reaction that has transformed our cultural life. Perhaps the most radical change of all is that we should accept change as a normal condition. In the days of Neo-Classicism the belief in ideal beauty and harmony still implied a goal which, once achieved, would permit no further artistic search. Today there is no general goal, unless it be that of free individual expression, and while we are familiar with the grouping and regrouping of artists willing to share an aesthetic idiom or a view of society, we are conscious of the lack of an all-embracing faith or vision that will bring a degree of unison into artistic creation to replace the patricide and fratricide that we accept as a normal part of modern self-determination in art. Such a faith cannot be manufactured, nor will bewailing our lack of it bring it more swiftly.

Meanwhile let us count our blessings. Art is a necessary and normal means of human expression. Do what he will, even the most individualistic amongst us is unable to shed his membership of mankind, and all his work is determined by values and functions which he shares with the rest of us. If the art of our age lacks the consolidating keystone of faith, it is none the less based on common ground. The strangeness of much modern art would at once disappear if we remembered its inescapably human origin.

If our century has failed to evolve a common structure of aims and values, some of its achievements have strikingly informed our art. The dramatic advances of modern science and the increasingly mechanistic character of our daily environment have necessarily left their mark on the content and idiom of art. Many artists, whether educated in scientific matters or not, have felt and emphasised a sense of kinship with the researching scientist, and their work has revealed an instinctive awareness of the changing picture of the world constructed by physicists and bio-chemists. Similarly the hypotheses of modern psychology have found echoes in art, just as philosophical theories have provoked artistic responses on many sides. Without any special knowledge of Einstein's theories the Cubists gave form to new concepts of space and time associated with him. The enthusiastic acceptance of modern technology characteristic of Futurism was taken up and made poetic by continuing generations of Constructivists. If Surrealism's use of Freudian theory seems curiously limited, all expressive art has benefited from the greater and more sympathetic insight into human actions that psychology has handed even to the most ignorant amongst us. Abstract Expressionist art seemed at its appearance directly influenced by Existentialist thought; subsequently it has sometimes looked as though Existentialist ideas had actually been plucked from the blossoming tree of modern art.

One of the most persisting specialities of modern art, a consciousness of space as something to be explored and exploited, is the property also of astronomers and schoolboys.

The place of art in our lives has changed drastically. From the church and the court, art has moved into the market place. Some of it is herded into public galleries, available to us all. Much of it, after a brief appearance on the stalls goes into private hands, but anyone living above subsistence level is in a position today to acquire the work of reputable artists in the form of drawings or prints. While there is little sign of a general interest in art, art itself has become less exclusive and has thus paralleled the marvellous social advances of our time.

The role and image of the artist himself has also changed, for we have witnessed a complete transformation of the avant-garde. Today the artist is neither the mysterious soothsayer nor the spurned outsider crying in the wilderness. More and more he has taken on professional status. Having once devoted a good part of his efforts to surviving the disdain of the public, the avant-garde artist today has to guard his integrity against the dangers inherent in success and publicity. The academies stand in the shadows while the limelight shines on successive waves of new and often very young artists, most of whom occupy the stage only briefly. Thesis is followed by antithesis; for synthesis there is no time. The danger in this situation does not lie in the rapid obsolescence of modes of art that yesterday seemed vital—the true work of art will survive in spite of this—but in a new academy of rebelliousness. To be new is the conventionality of our time. Not only is it easier to be new than to be good; it is also easier to be thrilled by the new than by the good.

The individual spectator, like the individual artist, has to find his way through a kaleidoscopic jungle of modern art. In a confused and fragmented world he cannot expect to find a neat and predigested world of art. Any knowledge of the art of the past and particularly of the recent past will help him to develop a sense of direction, but ultimately there is no substitute for his own developed sensibility. There can be little doubt that when, in some future age, the art of our time is measured against the art of the past, it will be found remarkable not so much for its inherent rebelliousness and self-questioning as for its ceaseless investigation into the potency of its means. In figurative and non-figurative art we have witnessed an ever sharpening awareness of the value of colour, line, form, scale and size, space and movement, both in their purely sensory effectiveness and as vehicles of emotion, and this will be recognised as an enduring contribution.

It has always taken time for cultural developments to reach people at large and it may be questionable whether the general public will ever feel the love for art which must be the basis for real understanding of it. We are told that our culture is moving from a verbal period into one of visual communication, which means that the requirements of normal living will demand a refinement of our visual awareness. The art of the last hundred years will be recognised as the great pioneer activity towards this refinement, and thus as the necessary and profoundly beneficial pursuit that some of us know it to have been.

Further Reading List

Alley, Ronald, *Gauguin*. London, Spring Books, 1961

Alloway, Lawrence, *Nine Abstract Artists: Their Work and Theory*. London, Tiranti, 1954

Banham, Reyner, *Theory and Design in the First Machine Age*. London Architectural Press, 1960

Barr, Alfred H., Jr., *Cubism and Abstract Art*. New York, Museum of Modern Art, 1936

Barr, Alfred H., Jr., *Fantastic Art, Dada, Surrealism* 3 ed. New York, Museum of Modern Art & Simon and Schuster, 1947

Barr, Alfred H., Jr., *German Painting and Sculpture*. New York, Museum of Modern Art, 1931

Barr, Alfred H., Jr., (ed.), *Masters of Modern Art*. New York, Museum of Modern Art & Simon and Schuster, 1954

Barr, Alfred H., Jr., *Henri Matisse, His Art and His Public*. New York, Museum of Modern Art, 1951

Barr, Alfred H., Jr., *Picasso: Fifty Years of His Art*. New York, Museum of Modern Art, 1946

Baur, John I.H., (ed.), *New Art in America: Fifty Painters of the 20th Century*. Greenwich, Conn., New York Graphic Society; New York, Praeger, 1957

Bayer, Herbert (& others), *Bauhaus 1919–1928*. Edited by Herbert Bayer, Walter Gropius, Ise Gropius. New York, Museum of Modern Art, 1938

Bertram, Anthony, *A Century of British Painting, 1851–1951*. London and New York, Studio, 1951

Blake, Peter, *The Master Builders*. London, Gollancz, 1960

Boase, T. S. R., *English Art 1800–1870*. Oxford, Clarendon Press, 1959

Boeck, Wilhelm & Sabartes, Jaime, *Picasso*. New York & Amsterdam, Abrams, 1955

Cassou, Jean; Langui, Emile & Pevsner, Nikolaus, *The Sources of Modern Art*. London, Thames & Hudson, 1962

Clark, Kenneth, *Landscape into Art*. London, Murray, 1949

Documents of Modern Art, Director: Robert Motherwell. New York, Wittenborn, Schultz, 1944 onwards

Elsen, Albert E., *Rodin*. New York, Museum of Modern Art, 1963

Evans, Joan, *John Ruskin*. London, Cape, 1954

Finberg, A. J., *The Life of J. M. W. Turner, R. A.* Oxford, Clarendon Press, 1961

Friedlaender, Walter, *David to Delacroix*. Cambridge, Harvard U.P. 1952

Gauss, Edward C., *The Aesthetic Theories of French Artists*. Baltimore, Johns Hopkins Press, 1949

Giedion, Sigfried, (ed.) *C.I.A.M.: A Decade of New Architecture*. 2 ed. New York, Wittenborn, 1954

Giedion, Sigfried, *Walter Gropius: Work and Teamwork*. New York, Reinhold, 1954

Giedion, Sigfried, *Space, Time and Architecture: The Growth of a New Tradition*. 3 ed. Cambridge, Harvard University, 1954

Giedion-Welcker, Carola, *Contemporary Sculpture: an Evolution in Volume and Space*. New York, Wittenborn, 1955

Golding, John, *Cubism*. London, Faber and Faber, 1959

Goldwater, Robert, *Gauguin*. New York, Abrams, 1957

Goldwater, Robert J., *Primitivism in Modern Painting*. New York and London, Harper, 1938

Goldwater, Robert J. & Treves, Marco, ed., *Artists on Art*. 2 ed. New York, Pantheon, 1947

Gray, Camilla, *The Great Experiment: Russian Art 1863–1922*. London, Thames & Hudson, 1962

Gray, Christopher, *Cubist Aesthetic Theories*. Baltimore, Johns Hopkins, 1953

Grohmann, Will, *Wassily Kandinsky*. New York, Abrams; Cologne, Dumont Schauberg, 1958

Grohman, Will, *Paul Klee*. New York, Abrams, 1954

Haftmann, Werner, *Malerei im 20. Jahrhundert*. 2 vol. Munich, Prestel, 1954–1955

Haftmann, Werner, *The Mind and Work of Paul Klee*. London, Faber and Faber, 1954

Hamilton, George H., *Manet and His Critics*. New Haven Yale University Press, 1954

Hamlin, Talbot, *Architecture Through the Ages*. New York, Putman, 1953

Händler, Gerhard, *German Painting in our Time*. Berlin, Rembrandt, 1956

Hatje, Gerd (gen. ed.), *Encyclopaedia of Modern Architecture*. London, Thames & Hudson, 1963

Herbert, Robert L. (ed.), *The Art Criticism of John Ruskin*. New York, Doubleday, 1964

Herbert, Robert L., *Barbizon Revisited*. Boston, Museum of Fine Arts, 1962

Herbert, Robert L. (ed.), *Modern Artists on Art*. Englewood Cliffs, New Jersey, Prentice-Hall, 1964

Hess, Thomas, *Abstract Painting, Background and American Phase*. New York, Viking Press, 1951

Hitchcock, Henry-Russell, *Architecture: Nineteenth and Twentieth Centuries*. Harmondsworth, Penguin Books, 1958

Hitchcock, Henry-Russell, *In the Nature of Materials 1887–1941: The Buildings of Frank Lloyd Wright*. New York, Duell, Sloan and Pearce, 1942; London, Elek, 1949

Howarth, Thomas, *Mackintosh and the Modern Movement*. London, Routledge and Kegan Paul, 1952

Hunter, Sam, *Modern American Painting and Sculpture*. 1900–1957. New York, Dell, 1958

Hunter, Sam, *Modern French Painting, 1855–1956*. New York, Dell, 1956

Huyghe, René, *Delacroix*. London, Thames & Hudson, 1963

Ironside, Robin, *Pre-Raphaelite Painters*. London, Phaidon, 1948

Jaffé, H. L. C., De Stijl 1917–1931, *The Dutch Contribution to Modern Art*. Amsterdam, Meulenhoff, 1956

Jean, Marcel, *The History of Surrealist Painting*. London, Weidenfeld & Nicholson, 1960

Jianou, Ionel, *Brancusi*. London, Adam Books, 1963

Johnson, Philip C., *Mies van der Rohe*. New York, The Museum of Modern Art, 1947

Kahnweiler, Daniel H., *Juan Gris, His Life and Work*. New York, Valentin, 1947

Kahnweiler, Daniel Henry, *The Sculptures of Picasso*. Photographs by Brassäi. London, Rodney Phillips, 1949

Lebel, Robert, *Marcel Duchamp*. London, Trianon, 1959

Le Corbusier (Charles-Edouard Jeanneret), *Towards a New Architecture*. London, Rodker; New York, Payson & Clarke, 1927

Leslie, C. R., *Memoirs of the Life of John Constable*. London, Phaidon, 1951

Lynton, Norbert, *Paul Klee*. London, Spring Books, 1964

Mack, Gerstle, *Paul Cézanne*. New York, Knopf, 1936

Mack, Gerstle, *Gustave Courbet*. New York, Knopf, 1951

Motherwell, Robert & Reinhardt, Ad, (eds), *Modern Artists in America: First Series*. New York, Wittenborn Schultz (1951)

Myers, Bernard, *The German Expressionists*. New York, Praeger, 1957

New York, Museum of Modern Art, *Built in U.S.A.: Post-War Architecture*. Edited by Henry-Russell Hitchcock and Arthur Drexler. New York, The Museum & Simon and Schuster, 1952

Novotny, Fritz, *Painting and Sculpture in Europe, 1780–1880*. Harmondsworth, Penguin Books, 1960

Olson, Ruther & Chanin, Abraham, *Naum Gabo, Antoine Pevsner*. Introduction by Herbert Read. New York, Museum of Modern Art, 1948

Pelles, Geraldine, *Art, Artists & Society*. Englewood Cliffs, New Jersey, Prentice-Hall, 1963

Penrose, Roland, *Picasso: His Life and Work*. London, Gollancz, 1958

Pevsner, Nikolaus, *Pioneers of the Modern Movement: from William Morris to Walter Gropius*. London, Faber and Faber, 1936

Pool, Phoebe, *Degas*. London, Spring Books, 1963

Ramsden, E. H., *Twentieth Century Sculpture*. London, Pleiades, 1949

Raynal, Maurice (& others), *History of Modern Painting*. 3 vol. Geneva, Skira, 1949–50

Read, Herbert, *A Concise History of Modern Painting*. London, Thames & Hudson, 1959

Read, Herbert, *Henry Moore, Sculpture and Drawings*. 2 vol. London, Lund Humphries, 1949–1956

Read, Herbert, *Ben Nicholson: Painting, Reliefs, Drawings*. London, Lund Humphries, 1948–1956

Read, Herbert, *The Philosophy of Modern Art*. New York, Horizon, 1953

Read, Herbert, (ed.), *Surrealism*. New York, Harcourt, Brace, 1936

Rewald, John, *Pierre Bonnard*. New York, Museum of Modern Art, 1948

Rewald, John, *Paul Cézanne*. London, Spring Books. n.d.

Rewald, John, *Degas Sculpture*. New York, Abrams, 1956

Rewald, John, *The History of Impressionism*. 2 ed. New York, Museum of Modern Art, 1955

Rewald, John, *Post-Impressionism from van Gogh to Gauguin*. New York, Museum of Modern Art, 1956

Rewald, John, *Georges Seurat*. 2 rev. ed. New York, Wittenborn, 1946

Richardson, John, *Edouard Manet*. London, Phaidon, 1958

Ritchie, Andrew Carnduff (ed.), *German Art of the Twentieth Century*. New York, Museum of Modern Art, 1957

Ritchie, Andrew C., (ed.), *German Art of the Twentieth Century*, by Werner Haftmann, Alfred Hentzen, William S. Lieberman. New York, Museum of Modern Art & Simon and Schuster, 1957

Ritchie, Andrew C., *Sculpture of the Twentieth Century*. New York, Museum of Modern Art, 1953

Robertson, Bryan, *Jackson Pollock*. London, Thames & Hudson, 1960

Rosenblum, Robert, *Cubism and Twentieth-Century Art*. London, Thames & Hudson, 1960

San Lazzaro, Gualtieri di., *Painting in France, 1895–1949*. New York, Philosophical Library, 1949

Schapiro, Meyer, *Vincent Van Gogh*. New York, Abrams, 1950

Seuphor, Michel, *Piet Mondrian: His Life and Work*. New York, Abrams, 1956

Soby, James T. & Barr, Alfred H., Jr., *Twentieth-Century Italian Art*. New York, Museum of Modern Art, 1949

Story, Somerville (intro.), *Rodin*. London, Phaidon, 1961

Sutton, Denys, *Nocturne: The Art of James McNeill Whistler*. London, Country Life, 1963

Sweeney, James J., *Alexander Calder*. 2 ed. rev. New York, Museum of Modern Art, 1951

The Taste of Our Time, New York, Skira, 1951-current

Whittick, Arnold, *European Architecture in the Twentieth Century*. London, Lockwood, 1950-in progress.

Whittick, Arnold, *Eric Mendelsohn*. 2 ed. London, Leonard Hill, 1956

Glossary

Abstract Expressionism. The more emotive form of abstract painting, pioneered by Kandinsky 1910–20, involving the more or less spontaneous exteriorisation of feelings in non-representational marks on canvas. Since 1945 there has been a considerable revival and extension of this process, first in the United States and subsequently wherever modern painting is practised. The term Action Painting is sometimes used to designate Abstract Expressionism when it is most dependent on physical movement on the part of the painter. [Pollock, de Kooning, Rothko, Mathieu]

Art Nouveau. The avant-garde style of the 1890s and the first years of this century, rooted in the painting of the 1880s but most effective in the fields of decorative and architectural design. The style is characterised by long, tenuous lines, often combined in patterns, and the avoidance of right-angles. It is specially important as the first non-historical style since Gothic times to win wide acceptance. [Mackintosh, van de Velde, Toorop]

Colour. Modern painting and design pay such close attention to colour that it is essential the basic terms used in discussing colour be understood. For classification purposes, colours have for some time been arranged to form the *colour circle.* The usual arrangement, mentioning only the *primary* and *secondary* colours, shows this sequence around the circle: yellow, orange, red, violet, blue, green, and back to yellow. In this system, yellow, red and blue are called the primaries: yellow + red + blue light = white; yellow + red + blue pigment = black. Orange, violet and green are the secondary colours and can be made by mixing two primaries: yellow + red = orange, etc. The colours diametrically opposite to each other across the circle (yellow and violet, red and green, blue and orange) are complementary to each other. Because of the functioning of our retinas, these colours enhance each other's vividness when juxtaposed and cancel each other out when mixed. Colours vary principally in hue and tone: the *hue* or tint refers to the particular colour or its position on the circumference of the circle, while *tone* refers to its lightness or darkness; that is, the quantity of white or black in it. Colours also vary in intensity, both in themselves and through their relationships with other colours, and also in their expressive character, which presumably relates to associational meanings we instinctively attach to them.

Constructivism. A movement in sculpture, initiated by the Russian artist Tatlin, 1913–4, in which sculpture is produced by assembling pieces of various materials in abstract spatial relationships. [Gabo, Pevsner]

Cubism. A movement that began in French painting during the years immediately succeeding the death of Cézanne (1906), first in the work of Picasso and Braque, and soon in the work of less closely related artists such as Delaunay, Villon, Gris, etc. The first phase of Picasso and Braque's Cubism is known as *Analytical* because of the fragmentation of objects on which it is founded; their second phase is known as *Synthetic* and involved a juxtaposing and superimposing of coloured forms to suggest objects. In many different ways, the Cubism of Picasso and Braque and the various interpretations of Cubism by other artists, in sculpture as well as painting, have provided the starting point for modern art movements all over the Western World.

De Stijl. Name of a Dutch art movement and of the journal in which its ideas were promulgated. It was founded by Mondrian, van Doesburg and van der Leck in 1917, and it was an extreme form of Elementarism, requiring artists and designers to limit themselves to rectangles, rectangular formal relationships, the primary colours, and black, grey and white.

Elementarism. A term sometimes used to embrace the various early twentieth-century movements (like Suprematism and De Stijl) that were founded on basic elements of form and colour. There was also a movement called Elementarism, founded by van Doesburg in 1925 as an extension and partial rejection of De Stijl principles.

Etching. The graphic process of biting a design into a metal plate with acid, and the print made from such a plate.

Expressionism. In general terms, expressionism involves the artistic transformation or distortion of the appearance of things in order to exploit them as a vehicle for emotive content. As a movement, Expressionism flourished mostly in Central Europe during the first three decades of this century, though individual Expressionist painters of significance may be found elsewhere. See also **Abstract Expressionism.** [Kirchner, Kokoschka, Kandinsky, Soutine]

Fauvism. A French movement in painting, centred on Matisse, marked by the use of intense and often unnaturalistic colour for the sake of poetic or dramatic expressiveness. The movement was named, on the occasion of its adherents' first public showing in 1905, by a critic who referred to the painters as *fauves* (wild beasts). [Dufy, Derain, Vlaminck]

Futurism. An Italian movement of wide influence, born in 1909 and in effect terminated by the first World War, insisting on and to some extent demonstrating new ideas in poetry, painting, sculpture, architecture, typography, etc. The Futurists disdained all forms of conservatism and attached themselves to the new world of technological power, speed, violence and efficiency, and sought to express in their works the complex of sensation and emotion of modern urban man. [Boccioni, Balla, Cara]

Hard-Edge. A name for a style of (normally) abstract painting involving clearly and severely defined areas of colour set in contrast against each other. As a movement Hard-Edge painting originated in the United States in the mid-1950s. [Ellsworth, Kelly, Feirelson]

Impressionism. The movement in painting associated with Monet (one of whose paintings gave the movement its name), Renoir, Pissaro, Sisley and others, most active in France during the 1870s and 1880s and of wide influence over Western art generally during the following decades. Founded on the observing of light and colour as they appear in nature, rather than on the accurate representation of forms as they are known to experience, Impressionist painting involved new techniques for swift notation and vividness. In this way, and in its attachment to plebeian and unintellectual subject matter, Impressionism was recognised as an assault on the principles of high art enshrined in the academies. Long denounced as a display of incompetence and charlatanism, today it is probably the most widely enjoyed phase in the history of painting.

International style. A term used chiefly for the architectural idiom that was born out of meeting of concrete building techniques with the stylistic ideals of Elementarism. The term stresses the wide acceptance of that idiom during the 1930s, often at the expense of more individual and regional qualities.

Lithography. A form of print-making, invented in 1798, in which designs made of specially prepared stones (or zinc plates) are transferred to paper. Drawing on the stone is a much freer process than that allowed by the other graphic media, and the use of more than one stone permits the use of several colours. One of the special characteristics of Lithography is the delicate flatness of the areas of colour printed in this way; this was of particular attraction to such artists as Toulouse-Lautrec, Bonnard and Vuillard, as well as to Art Nouveau and later artists generally.

Machine Aesthetic. A phrase used to refer to the taste for forms suggestive of machinery that characterised much avant-garde art and design in the 1920s and was often justified in theory by talk of functionalism.

Matter Painting. A term used to describe recent forms of painting exploiting particularly thick media. [Dubuffet, Tapies]

Neo-Classicism. The sudden and rapid growth of antiquarian knowledge, and the search for an artistic idiom marked by clarity, seriousness and high idealism, brought a wave of classicism towards the end of the 18th century which continued well into the 19th century and is associated primarily with the work of David, Canova, Schinkel and Soane.

Neo-Impressionism. The movement associated with Seurat and Signac, involving an exceptionally scientific use of unmixed colours in close juxtaposition to give the effect of colours observed by the artist. By a method known as *Divisionism* the painter split up observed colours into their primary and secondary constituents, these he set down in small dots—a process known as pointillism—so that, when seen from a proper distance, the dots of colour would seem to merge without the loss of vividness and accuracy that less controlled techniques could involve. As the name implies, this amounted to an extension, as well as a criticism, of Impressionism.

Op Art. i.e. Optical Art, referring to the recent exploitation, mostly in painting, of the effects of retinal overstimulation through calculated confrontations of colour and contrasts. [Vasarely, Riley]

Pop Art. An art movement of the last few years characterised by borrowing motifs and stylistic devices from the world of mass media (advertising, comic strips, packaging, etc.). On the whole, Pop Art seems both to celebrate the visual qualities of these motifs and to satirise a world that surrounds itself with these things while insisting on its superiority to them.

Post-Impressionism. General term for the various reactions against Impressionism, and extensions of it, in French painting. Post-Impressionism does not represent a movement, but rather a period and an attitude. The leading Post-Impressionists were Cézanne, Seurat, Gauguin and van Gogh.

Ready-made. Marcel Duchamp's term for a found object which the artist adopts and exhibits, unaltered, as a work of art.

Romanticism. The first wave of emotional, introspective and often unrealistic art, associated with such men as Goya, Blake and Delacroix; also the period in which this happened (say, 1790 to 1840), and the wide range of creativity in which comparable subjectivism and emotionalism may be found (Beethoven, Berlioz, Byron, Shelley, etc.).

Suprematism. A Russian movement in painting, initiated by Malevich in 1915, placing great emphasis on the sensations communicated by the simplest forms and colours painted on a white canvas.

Surrealism. An international movement in literature and art that emerged in Paris in the early 1920s (first Surrealist manifesto, 1924), presented fantasy images supposedly brought out of the artists' subconscious, and sometimes exploring techniques of automatic (i.e. consciously uncontrolled) painting to produce accidental images and effects likely to stimulate the imagination. [Ernst, Dali, Magritte, Masson]

Symbolism. A French movement, principally literary, that flourished in the 1880s (it was named in 1886). A reaction against the realism of the preceding decades, Symbolism was characterised by an attempt to unify the inner and outer worlds through a patently subjective handling of objective matter, and by a belief in the communicative power of the musical qualities of words, forms and colours. In France Symbolism in literature was associated principally with Mallarmé, Rimbaud and Verlaine; Maeterlinck, George, Rilke, Yeats and others, carried it into other countries and into this century. In painting Symbolism was part of the reaction against Impressionism: Gauguin, Bernard, Denis, Redon and others may be described as Symbolists artists. Art Nouveau owes many of its qualities to the experiments of the Symbolists.

Index

The numbers in heavy type refer to colour plates; italic numbers refer to black and white illustrations.

174

Acknowledgements

The Publishers gratefully acknowledge the consent of the following for permission to reproduce subjects illustrated in this book:

© S.P.A.D.E.M., Paris, 1965. *Colour:* 12, 17, 22, 24, 25, 26, 29, 31, 33, 34, 35, 36, 37, 46, 47, 48, 49, 53, 54, 58, 69, 75, 81, 102. *Black and white:* 17, 20, 21, 22, 39, 41, 43, 44, 45, 61, 66, and illustration on p. 7.

© A.D.A.G.P., *Colour:* 50, 51, 55, 57, 61, 70, 71, 74, 86, 87, 98. *Black and white:* 70, 71, 81.

© SABAM, Brussels. *Colour:* 76.

© Roman Norbert Ketterer, Campione d'Italia. *Colour:* 59, 60.

© VEB.E.A. Seeman, Leipzig. *Colour:* 41.

© Nachlassverwaltung Franz Marc. *Colour:* 62.

© Paul Nash Trust. *Colour:* 79.

Photographs were provided by the following:

Colour: A.C.L., Brussels 76; Stedelijk Museum, Amsterdam 63, 83; Museum of Modern Art, Antwerp 38; Kunstmuseum, Basle 58; National Galerie, East Berlin 16, 41; Staatsgemäldesammlungen, Berlin-Dahlem 22; Berne Kunstmuseum 81; Galerie Beyeler, Basel 78; J. Blaucl, Munich 62; Hedrich Blessing, Chicago 84; Boston Museum of Fine Arts 31, 33; J. Camponogara, Lyon 27; A. Caro, London 110; Leo Castelli Gallery, New York 107, 108; Art Institute, Chicago 28, 51; The Royal Museum of Fine Arts, Copenhagen 46; R. Descharnes, Paris 72; Doeser Photos, Laren, Holland 82; W. Drayer, Zurich 74; J. R. Dunlop, Washington 26, 87; R. Einzig, London 113; Gimpel Fils, London 89; Giraudon, Paris 57; J. J. de Goede, Holland 35; Georges Groc, Alri 36; Hanover Gallery, London 98; Edits Hazan, Paris 54; L. Herve, Paris 111; J. Heienberg, Bergen 39; H. Hinz, Basle 50, 52, 75; M. Holford, London 1, 2, 3, 4, 5, 7, 8, 9, 10, 11, 12, 13, 15, 17, 18, 19, 20, 23, 24, 25, 29, 37, 40, 43, 53, 69, 71, 73, 77, 79, 85, 88, 93, 97, 100, 101, 102, 103, 104, 105, 106; D. Hughes-Gilbey, London 95; J. Hyde, Paris 14; Kasmin Gallery, London 109; Tom Kay, London 112; J. Klima Jr. Detroit 42; The Courtauld Institute of Art, London 30; Lords Gallery, London 68; Marlborough Fine Arts, London 96; Mas, Barcelona 6, 45; E. Meyer, Vienna 44, 60; The Museum of Modern Art, New York 48, 49, 65, 66, 90, 92; S. R. Guggenheim Museum, New York 55, 61; R. Nickel, Park Ridge, Illinois 86; Prof. A. Roth, Zürich 67; The San Francisco Museum of Art 91; Elton Schnellbacher, Pittsburgh 47; Sherwin Greenberg Studios, Buffalo, New York 70; Silvana Editoriale, Milan 56; H. Stickelmann, Bremen 59; D. Swann, London 21; Mr and Mrs Burton Tremaine, Meridon, Connecticut 80; H. Weitman, Washington, St Louis 94; A. J. Wyatt, Philadelphia 34, 64; Kunstgewerbemuseum, Zurich 32.

Black and white: Foto Commissie Rijksmuseum, Amsterdam 19; Stedelijk Museum, Amsterdam 63; Anderson/Giraudon, Paris 7; Wayne Andrews, Detroit 29, 31; T. R. Annan, Glasgow 37, 38; Architectural Review, Y. Futagawa, London 89; Archives Photographiques, Paris 9; Öffentliche Kunstsammlung, Basle 81; Bauhaus Archiv, Darmstadt 76; Kunstgeschichtliche Bildstelle, Humboldt Universität zu Berlin 13; Photographische Abteilung, Staatliche Museen zu Berlin 23; Kunstmuseum, Berne 41; Max Bill, Zurich 79, 84; Boudot-Lamotte, Paris 36; Busch-Reisinger Museum, Cambridge, Massachusetts 64; Chevojon, Paris 30, 53, 66; Art Institute, Chicago, illustration on p. 7; Chicago Architectural Photographing Company 35; Musei Civici, Como 59; Ny Carlsberg Glyptotek, Copenhagen 10; Galerie Creuzevault, Paris 82; Mme. van Doesburg, Meudon 60; Kunstmuseum, Düsseldorf 49; Dyckerhoff & Widmann, Munich 58; John Ebstel, New York 91; Fox Photos, London 16; French Government Tourist Office, London 28;

Alexander Georges, Pomona, New York 86; Giraudon, Paris 1, 11; Camilla Gray, London 56, 78; Grosvenor Gallery, London 65; Hedrich/Blessing, Chicago 87; L. Herve, Paris 54, 73, 74; Hirshorn Collection, New York 70; M. Holford, London 17, 20, 21; A. F. Kersting, London 15, 32; Sir G. Keynes, London 4; G. E. Kidder Smith, New York 90; Leco Photo Service, New York 80; British Museum, London 3, 5; National Buildings Record, London 25, 34; National Film Archives, London 42; Royal Institute of British Architects, London 33; Sir John Soane Museum, London 14; Tate Gallery, London 22, 52; Man Ray, Paris 47; Photo Marburg, Marburg, Germany 27; Marlborough Fine Arts, London 69; Marlborough New London, London 50; The Museum of Modern Art, New York 39, 43, 44, 45, 48, 51, 55, 61, 67, 68, 72, 75, 83, 85; S. R. Guggenheim, Museum, New York 71, 88; E. M. Van Ojen, The Hague 77; Bibliothèque Nationale, Paris 6, 12; Mario Perotti, Edizione del Milione, Milan 24; Mme. A. Pevsner, Paris 62; Philadelphia Museum of Art 40; Radio Times Hulton Picture Library, London 26; Dr. O. Reinhardt, Winterthur 18; Service de Documentation Photographique, Paris 2; Dr. F. Stoedtner, Düsseldorf 57; Tretyakov Gallery, Moscow 46; Josiah Wedgwood & Sons Ltd., Stoke-on-Trent 8.

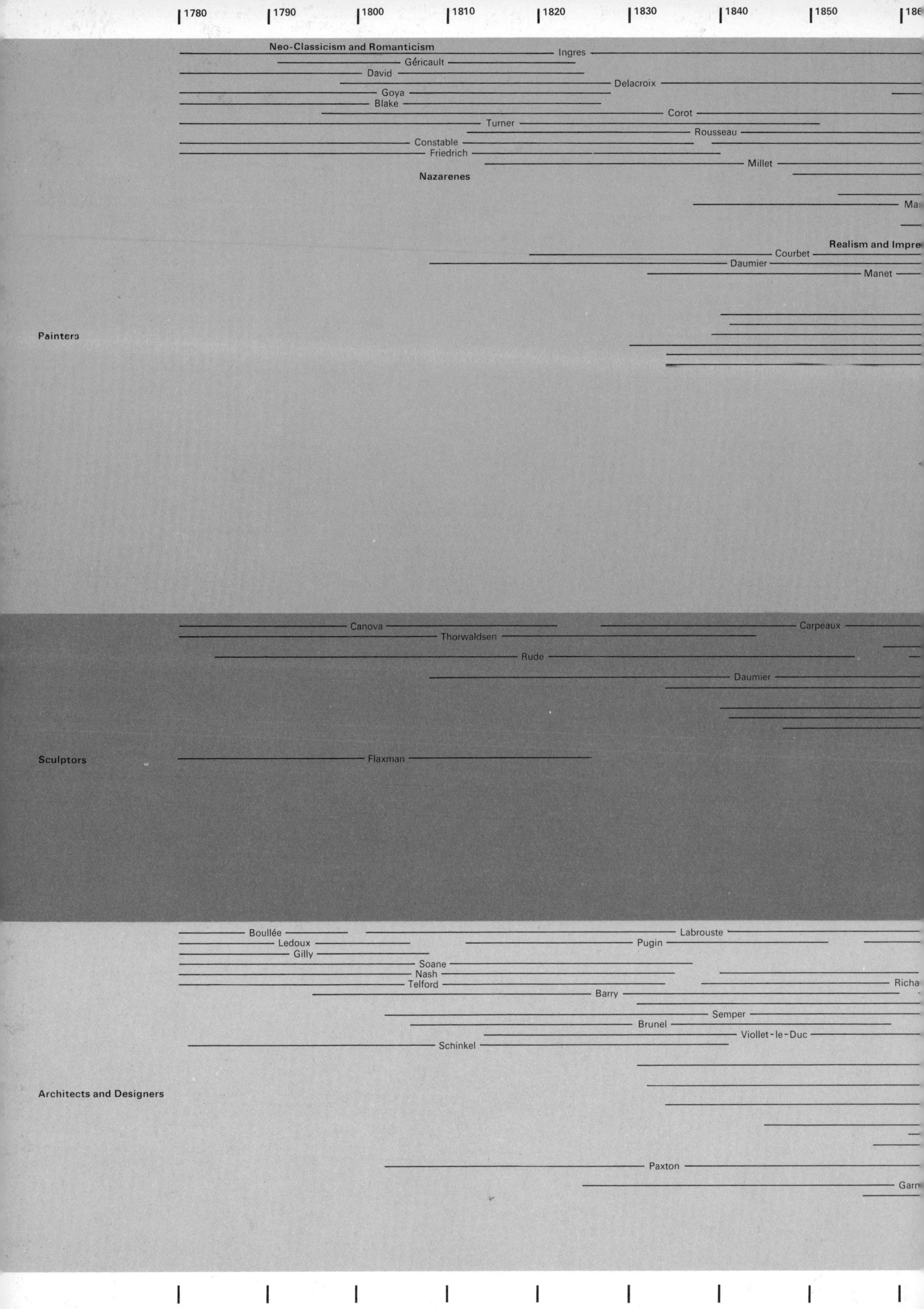

Neo-Classicism and Romanticism

Ingres

Géricault

David

Delacroix

Goya

Blake

Corot

Turner

Rousseau

Constable

Friedrich

Millet

Nazarenes

Ma

Realism and Impre

Courbet

Daumier

Manet

Painters

Sculptors

Canova

Thorwaldsen

Carpeaux

Rude

Daumier

Flaxman

Architects and Designers

Boullée

Labrouste

Ledoux

Pugin

Gilly

Soane

Nash

Richa

Telford

Barry

Semper

Brunel

Viollet-le-Duc

Schinkel

Paxton

Garr